WHAT'S THE USE OF PHILOSOPHY?

WHAT'S THE USE
OF PHILOSOPHY?

Philip Kitcher

OXFORD
UNIVERSITY PRESS

OXFORD
UNIVERSITY PRESS

Oxford University Press is a department of the University of Oxford. It furthers
the University's objective of excellence in research, scholarship, and education
by publishing worldwide. Oxford is a registered trade mark of Oxford University
Press in the UK and certain other countries.

Published in the United States of America by Oxford University Press
198 Madison Avenue, New York, NY 10016, United States of America.

Library of Congress Cataloging-in-Publication Data
Names: Kitcher, Philip, 1947– author.
Title: What's the use of philosophy? / Philip Kitcher.
Description: New York, NY, United States of America :
Oxford University Press, [2023] |
Includes bibliographical references and index. |
Identifiers: LCCN 2022040696 (print) | LCCN 2022040697 (ebook) |
ISBN 9780197657249 (h/b) | ISBN 9780197657263 (epub) |
ISBN 9780197657270
Subjects: LCSH: Philosophy—Introductions.
Classification: LCC B103 .K58 2023 (print) | LCC B103 (ebook) |
DDC 100—dc23/eng/20220922
LC record available at https://lccn.loc.gov/2022040696
LC ebook record available at https://lccn.loc.gov/2022040697

DOI: 10.1093/oso/9780197657249.001.0001

Printed by Sheridan Books, Inc., United States of America

To the wonderful graduate students
whom I have had the privilege of teaching
—

and for all the others
who once fell in love with philosophy
and who would like the relationship
to stay that way

CONTENTS

PREFACE

Occasionally, the question posed in my title is asked as if the questioner eagerly expected an answer. For the most part, however, the speaker's tone—heavily emphatic on the "use" and the "philosophy"—suggests something quite different. That the question is unanswerable. Because, as everybody knows, philosophy is utterly useless.

For the past twenty years or so, I have been brooding about the question. The usual dismissive tone is, I believe, readily understandable. It stems from the remoteness of philosophy from the rest of contemporary culture. Philosophers appear to outsiders as peculiar beings, perhaps highly intelligent but with bizarre tastes in the ways they spend their "work" time. They labor over questions without answering them, spend hours in heated debates about very little (if anything), criticize one another with peculiar, and often distasteful, ferocity. Their employers, mostly colleges and universities, pay them for engaging in their pointless jousts. But even their colleagues, who teach and do research in other academic disciplines, seem to agree with the general judgment that their activities are incomprehensible.

During the early years of this century, I became more and more convinced that this worrying attitude was common enough to deserve attention. The Humanities rarely receive much respect in the English-speaking world. Philosophy is usually assigned to this low-status division, but it is almost always cut off from its fellow orphans. Once, of course, philosophers were avidly read by excited members of the public. Their works were treasured as sources of life-changing transitions in allegiances and attitudes. Not anymore. Even in the days when there were local bookshops, the philosophy section was typically stocked with works few Anglophone philosophers would recognize as contributions to their discipline. What has happened to philosophy?

I began to focus my unease about this situation when Armen Marsoobian, the editor of *Metaphilosophy*, invited me to a conference in London to celebrate the fortieth anniversary of the journal. Four speakers, of whom I was one, presented their perspectives on the state of the subject. My contribution was the first draft of Chapter 1 in this volume, later revised and published with the other papers in an issue of *Metaphilosophy*. That issue did not include any parts of the lively panel discussion.

I had expected criticism, even hostility, and I received some of the former; I don't recall any of the latter (perhaps repression has done its impressive work). But I was also surprised by a fair amount of sympathy for my heterodox position. Besides that, what remains in my memory is a vigorous debate with Timothy Williamson (surely one of the most distinguished philosophers of his generation.) It was conducted in that wonderful spirit of old-fashioned disagreement that used to be a characteristically British style of intellectual exchange. No quarter given, but everyone goes off happily to the pub afterward. In this instance, we retired to an excellent dinner.

Reactions to the published article convinced me that I was far from alone in worrying about the current state of Anglophone philosophy. Before long, Rob Tempio, philosophy editor for Princeton University Press, had written to me with the suggestion that I expand the article as a short book. I mentioned that possibility to Peter Ohlin, my long-time editor at Oxford University Press, and someone I count as a friend. Peter, too, thought this was a good suggestion, although, like me, he was concerned about poaching another editor's bright idea. In any event, the issue was moot. I did not feel ready to write a book in this area.

A few years later, Stefan Hartmann and Michela Massimi invited me to give a keynote address at the meeting of the European Society for the Philosophy of Science (later published in the *European Journal for the Philosophy of Science*). I accepted with alacrity. Wishing to develop my approach further, I wrote a preliminary version of Chapter 2. When I delivered it at the conference, I was again pleasantly surprised by a sense that what I had said had resonated with at least some parts of the large audience. The discussion opened with a question that has occupied me ever since. It was posed by a young woman whose name I do not know. She began by saying that she was sympathetic to the approach I had taken—but she wondered how people like herself, starting out on their philosophical careers, could pursue something of that sort in a profession whose priorities ran counter to the kinds of philosophy I commended.

Similar reactions greeted the John Dewey Lecture I delivered (via Zoom) to the 2021 meeting of the Eastern Division of the American Philosophical Association (subsequently published in the *Proceedings* of the Association). Both during the discussion immediately following my presentation, and in emails I received during the next few days, younger philosophers again pressed me on how they might actually pursue the kinds of philosophy that appealed to them—without ruining their careers. I tried to respond, always with a definite feeling that what I was saying was inadequate.

It seemed, then, that the time had come to attempt to develop my thoughts further, to combine and integrate the sometimes scattered pieces of the three lectures, to supplement them with further material to make some of my negative and positive points clearer, and to address more systematically the worry that, at least for younger philosophers, following anything like the course I described would be suicidal.

I wanted to write a book that would not only expose the insights in the common, rhetorical version of my title question— but also respond to those who eagerly want an answer. What follows is my attempt to do that.

Chapters 1 and 2 are revised versions of the published articles with the same titles. They have been rewritten to reflect small adjustments in my views, to make them more broadly accessible, and to integrate them with one another and the chapters that follow them. The third chapter is new. Its presence reflects my sense that, besides the impressionistic surveys of its predecessors, a systematic diagnosis of the shortcomings of much contemporary Anglophone philosophy would help to expose what has gone wrong. The fourth is a considerably expanded presentation of my positive conception of philosophy as outlined in my Dewey lecture—my response to the imagined eager questioner, who is genuinely open to an answer. The task assigned to a Dewey lecturer is to offer some mix of intellectual autobiography and reflections on the state of the profession. I have eliminated the former, and developed considerably further the core themes of the latter, since I believe I can now be somewhat more precise about what I have in mind. The final chapter is written to that first questioner who responded to the first version of Chapter 2, and to all her successors who have voiced similar concerns. I hope it is more helpful than what I have previously said to them.

In making my negative case, the principal focus is on genres, and I have tried to avoid pointing fingers at individual philosophers. Only in a very few instances is identification unavoidable. Fortunately, in these cases, the people most prominent either in pioneering or developing the style of philosophy I criticize nevertheless deserve respect and even admiration. Their practices, although flawed, have an art, a sensitivity, and an intelligence that is often lacking in those who imitate them.

Where I identify healthy growth in current philosophical endeavors, I try to single out examples, in hopes that they will be useful to the reader. So I drop a fair number of names. My lists of positive figures should not be taken to indicate that those whom I single out are the *only* shining lights in the areas of philosophy with which I associate them. Or even that they are the *prime* examples for making my point. Others might choose differently. Quite reasonably, too.

My emphasis throughout is on the use (or uselessness) of *philosophy*, a discipline practiced in a variety of ways for well over two millennia. Only in the final chapter do I take up (briefly) a different question, the potential usefulness of *philosophers*. Many outsiders who find the subject arid and irrelevant might well agree that the subject's practitioners do some valuable work. Although philosophers show an odd devotion to wrestling with unanswerable questions lacking any practical import, the effort breeds in them skills for lucid and rigorous thinking. To be sure, when they do their "creative research," their talents are misapplied. Sometimes, however, earning their pay requires them to stand up in front of a previously uninitiated audience and hold forth. When they do that, they often help those who listen to them to think more clearly. Since most of their hearers leave their presence without becoming addicted to the sterile game playing that occupies the consummate professional philosopher's "research" life, the listeners tend to put their newly acquired capacities to work in productive ways. As, perhaps, do the philosophers at the times when they are off-duty and pondering some important decision.

This side of a philosopher's life will occupy me only in the final chapter, where I shall offer some thoughts on the importance of teaching, and on the contexts in which introducing people to the subject might prove valuable. "What's the use of *philosophers*?" has a relatively straightforward answer (just summarized). Having spent fifty-odd years devoting myself to the subject, I don't believe the answer can simply be extended to resolve my title question. "Philosophy's use is to provide material for training people, who can then use the material to help others to think better than they would otherwise have done" won't do. My imagined eager questioner wants more than that: a valuable role for some of the books and articles philosophers write. So do I.

I am extremely grateful to Armen Marsoobian, Stefan Hartmann, Michela Massimi, and the Committee on Lectures and Publications of the American Philosophical Association for the invitations that spurred me to write the raw material for three of these chapters. I am also indebted to Natalia Rogach Alexander, Nancy Cartwright, Lorraine Daston, Justin Clarke-Doane, John Dupré, Gerd Gigerenzer, Clark Glymour, Robbie Kubala, Susan Neiman, Alexander Rosenberg, James Woodward, and two anonymous readers of an earlier draft, all of whom have given me thoughtful advice about how to improve it. Rob Tempio deserves thanks for his magnanimity and forbearance in not insisting that planting a seed secured the right to the unpredictable fruits that have emerged from a decade in which many people, most especially those who have responded to those original lectures, have done a fair bit of weeding, watering, pruning, and fertilizing. Besides those I have already thanked, Peter Ohlin should be counted among the gardeners. I am indebted to him for much advice, help, and support.

I am grateful for permission to reprint revised versions of three published articles: to Armen Marsoobian and *Metaphilosophy* for allowing me to reuse large parts of "Philosophy Inside Out" (*Metaphilosophy* 42, no. 3 [2011]: 248–260); to the editors of the *European Journal for Philosophy of Science* and to Springer Publications for permission to include much of "So … Who *Is* Your Audience?" (*European Journal for Philosophy of Science* 9, no. 1 [2018]: 1–15); and to the Officers of the American Philosophical Association for allowing me to draw on "The Whole Function of Philosophy" (*Proceedings and Addresses of the American Philosophical Association* 95 [November 2021]: 84–102).

Finally, I want to thank all the students I have taught during a longish career, especially those whose doctoral dissertations I have supervised. They have inspired me to reflect on my profession and its value, and they have constantly challenged my assumptions. This book is for them and for the many others who will, I hope, keep the value of philosophy alive.

Autumn 2021
Berlin
February 2022
New York

PHILOSOPHY INSIDE OUT

Once upon a time, in a country not too far away, the most prominent musicians decided to become serious about their profession. They encouraged their promising students to devote hours to special exercises designed to strengthen fingers, shape lips, and extend breath control. Within a few years, conservatories began to hold exciting competitions, at which the most rigorous études would be performed in public. For a while, these contests went on side by side with concerts devoted to the traditional repertoire. Gradually, however, interest in the compositions of the past—and virtually all those of the present—began to wane. Serious pianists found the studies composed by Chopin, Liszt, Debussy, and Ligeti insufficiently taxing and dismissed the suites, concertos, and sonatas of Bach, Mozart, Beethoven, Brahms, Bartok, and Prokofiev as worthy of performance only by second-raters.

Popular interest in the festivals organized by the major conservatories quickly declined, although the contests continued to be attended by a tiny group of self-described cognoscenti. A few maverick musicians, including some who had once been counted

What's the Use of Philosophy? Philip Kitcher, Oxford University Press. © Oxford University Press 2023. DOI: 10.1093/oso/9780197657249.003.0001

among the serious professionals, offered performances of works their elite ex-colleagues despised. When reports of the broad enthusiastic response to a recital centered on the late Beethoven sonatas came to the ears of the professionals, the glowing reviews produced only a smile and a sniff. For serious pianists, the fact that one of their former fellows had now decided to slum it was no cause for concern. Compared to the recent competition in which one pianist had delivered *Multi-Scale 937* in under 7'10" and another had ornamented *Quadruple Tremolo 41* with an extra trill, an applauded performance of the *Hammerklavier* was truly small potatoes.

As time went on, the outside audience for "serious performance" dwindled to nothing, and the public applause for the "second-raters" who offered Bach, Chopin, and Messiaen became more intense. The smiles of the cognoscenti grew a little more strained, and the sniffs were ever more disdainful.

***

Is this sorry tale relevant to the current state of philosophy in the English-speaking world? I shall not try to offer conclusive reasons for thinking that it captures the predicament of Anglophone philosophy in the early twenty-first century—but I shall argue that philosophers, as well as members of the wider intellectual community and even reflective citizens, should worry about the question. "Reconstruction in philosophy" may be urgently needed.[1] I shall present a vision of the discipline questioning the dominant assumption that topics currently viewed as central deserve the emphasis placed on them, and celebrating issues often regarded as peripheral.

Reconstruction in Philosophy is the title of a book by John Dewey (Dewey 1920/1982), whom I take to be the most important philosopher of the twentieth century. The approach I shall elaborate renews Dewey's concerns with respect to our own times. To add to the madness of my estimate of Dewey's significance, let me start with his provocative characterization of philosophy:

> If we are willing to conceive education as the process of forming fundamental dispositions, intellectual and emotional, toward nature and fellow men, philosophy may even be defined *as the general theory of education*. (Dewey 1916/1980, 338)

Dewey's proposal reminds us of his pioneering work in setting up the lab school at the University of Chicago, and of his continual willingness to cross West 120th Street to join Columbia University to Teachers College (as well as pointing to his many-sided work in the world—can we imagine any philosopher selected to preside over the trial of an exiled political giant, the contemporary counterpart of Leon Trotsky?). For those who have been well brought up in recent Anglo-American philosophy, his suggested definition of philosophy is, at best, quaint. Applied philosophy is all very well, but we know where the center of the discipline lies: in metaphysics, epistemology, philosophy of language, and philosophy of mind—the "core areas" as aficionados today typically call them—in a coinage that has grown in prominence during the past decades and is increasingly used as a semantic weapon for down-grading certain kinds of work.

Yet why exactly should we accept that standard picture? What is philosophy supposed to do—for individual people or for a broader culture? Pragmatists will think of areas of inquiry as making contributions to human lives, and they will suppose that those areas are healthy only if they are directed toward delivering the things expected of them. When some discipline seems to be cut off from other fields, when the "literature" it produces is regarded as arcane and irrelevant, they will think it worth asking if that discipline is doing its proper job. Immediately after characterizing philosophy as the "general theory of education," Dewey buttresses his definition by raising this issue:

> Unless a philosophy is to remain symbolic—or verbal—or a sentimental indulgence for a few, or else mere arbitrary dogma, its auditing of past experience and its program of values must take effect in conduct. (Dewey 1916/1980, 338)

The danger that a field of inquiry will become a "sentimental indulgence for a few"—or perhaps a site of intellectual jousting for a few—is especially urgent in the case of philosophy.

> The fact that philosophical problems arise because of widespread and widely felt difficulties in social practice is disguised because philosophers become a specialized class which uses a technical language, unlike the vocabulary in which the direct difficulties are stated. (Dewey 1916/1980, 338)

Two important points are made here: first, philosophical problems emerge from situations in which people—many people, not just an elite class—find themselves; second, the development of technical language is particularly problematic in philosophy. Both these points need to be treated carefully.

Take the second first. Philosophy is hardly unique in using a specialized language. Mathematicians, physicists, and biologists all talk and write in ways outsiders find incomprehensible. Can the pragmatist suspicion that all is not well with the technicalia of philosophy be distinguished from the philistine dismissal of the esoterica of mathematics, physics, and molecular genetics? Or, for that matter, from the critical remarks analytic philosophers direct against the use of the language used in areas of the humanities for which they tend to have little esteem—literary theory, for example?

There are indeed important differences between philosophy and the practice of the natural sciences. Faced with skepticism about the worth of seeking the Higgs boson or investigating the concentrations of particular molecules in particular cells of apparently uninteresting organisms, particle physicists and molecular biologists can describe, at least in outline, a sequence of steps that will lead from answers to the technical questions they pose to issues of far broader, and more readily comprehensible significance. Investigations of these molecules can be combined with those achieved in different studies to yield a picture of a small step in the development of organisms, and that picture, in its turn, can be integrated with perspectives similarly achieved on other aspects of development, until, at last, our successors may understand how a multicellular organism emerges from a zygote. Not only is there a vision of how a large question, one whose significance outsiders can appreciate, can be decomposed into smaller issues, significant because of their potential contribution to giving the large answer, but there is every reason to believe that well-grounded answers can be found. Discovering those answers may require time, persistence, and ingenuity, but researchers are encouraged by the recognition that others have done similar things before. They see themselves as having "methods" for arriving at reliable results.

Philosophy isn't like that. To the extent that the technical issues that fill Anglophone journals result in any comprehensible way from questions of large significance, they do not seem to have reached the stage at which firm answers might be found. Any defense of the idea that philosophy, like particle physics and molecular biology, proceeds by the accumulation of reliable answers to technical questions would have to provide examples of consensus on which larger agreements are built. Yet, as the philosophical questions diminish in size, disagreement and controversy persist, new distinctions are drawn, and yet tinier issues are generated. Decomposition continues downward, until the interested community becomes too exhausted, too small, or too uninspired to play the game any further.

The phenomenon is especially dispiriting when industries of busywork descend from an original and powerful philosophical idea. Giants have sometimes walked the earth, even in the past few decades, bequeathing to their students and successors a new approach to some important cluster of topics. The immediately following generation often takes up the inspiration in fruitful ways, elaborating the pioneering perspective. Soon, however, "normal philosophy" takes over, fussing over minute details. Within philosophy, the illumination of the early discussions is dimmed by debates of increasingly decreasing significance. The larger world ignores those debates, and, in its deliberations, the power of the conception may live on—as with John Rawls's thought of the basic structure of society as decided in the original position (Rawls 1999)—even while the philosophers argue interminably about the exact thickness of the veil of ignorance.

Mathematics, rather than the natural sciences, might provide a more promising comparison, since there are affinities between the purest parts of mathematics and game playing, and some famous players have even gloried in the "uselessness" of the subject (Hardy 1967). Here, too, however, similar points hold. Even at their most playful, mathematical investigations have rules for bringing the game to an end; one may fail to see the point of a theorem (why anyone would care about it), but disputes about its status as a theorem can typically be settled. Furthermore, the alleged uselessness of pure mathematics should be placed in historical context. Until the Renaissance, mathematics was viewed as a low-status activity, precisely because its practitioners were perceived as playing games of no great significance. Developments of mathematics in the sixteenth and seventeenth centuries showed how mathematical languages, devised for esoteric purposes or for no purpose at all, might be valuable in framing physical inquiry. Talk of imaginary numbers, for instance, characterized apologetically by Bombelli (who introduced them) as "subtle and useless," became an integral part of an algebraic language for a nascent theory of functions that could be deployed in understanding motion. The role of mathematics within inquiry—and the social status of mathematicians—changed. In effect, from the seventeenth and eighteenth centuries on, mathematicians have been given license to focus on the questions they (collectively) regard as significant, to introduce new languages, and to find promising new games as they please. Workers in other fields can borrow from these languages in reformulating their own questions, and, even though not every extension of mathematics lends itself to appropriation by physicists or biologists or economists, there have been enough successful examples to justify the original faith in unanticipated fruits of free mathematical play. Hardy, distressed by the outbreak of World War II, gloried in the uselessness of number theory— and did not foresee how cryptography would later apply his field.

Philosophy might aspire to something similar, the framing of conceptions that can assist existing disciplines, or even initiate new modes of inquiry. At important moments in its history it has done just that, but its success has resulted from careful attention to features of the state of knowledge or of the broader human condition. There is no internal dynamic of building on and extending the problem solutions of a field that can be pursued in abstraction from other inquiries. In part that is because of the lack of procedures for yielding firm solutions, but also because philosophical issues evolve. As Dewey remarks of philosophical questions, "We do not solve them: we get over them" (Dewey 1909/1998, 14).

***

This feature of philosophy is central to the other point I mentioned above as worthy of careful treatment. It is easy to suppose that there are timeless questions, formulated by the Greeks, or by Descartes, or by Kant, or by Frege, or by Wittgenstein, that, once introduced, must constitute the core of the subject thenceforward. I want to suggest a different history, one more consonant with the pictures historians paint of the evolution of the natural and social sciences. Philosophy grows out of an impulse toward understanding nature and the human place in it, an impulse that was present long before the invention of writing. At early stages of written culture, that impulse was expressed in undifferentiated concerns about the cosmos, matter, life, society, and value. As Dewey remarks in the opening pages of *The Quest for Certainty*, the impetus to philosophy was present in all human contexts, from the natural and social environments of our Paleolithic ancestors, through the variant forms of society we know from history and anthropology, to the circumstances of the present. At each stage, the philosopher's first task is to recognize the appropriate questions that arise for his contemporaries. Dewey focuses this thought by offering a diagnosis of the needs of the 1920s:

> The problem of restoring integration and cooperation between man's beliefs about the world in which he lives and the values and purposes that should direct his conduct is the deepest problem of modern life. It is the problem of any philosophy that is not isolated from that life. (Dewey 1929/1988, 204)

Whether or not this is a good diagnosis for his time or for ours is something I'll consider later. For the moment, however, I want to see it as pointing to two axes along which philosophy has historically operated, and as recognizing an important shift along one of these.

For most of the history of the sciences, those most deeply involved saw themselves as doing "natural philosophy." Similarly, figures we continue to teach in philosophy classes recognized no limitations that prevented them from pronouncing on issues we take as scientific. From the fragments of their writings that have come down to us, the pre-Socratics were plainly concerned with questions of physics; Aristotle evidently took all nature as his province; Descartes wrote his discourse on method as a preface to treatises on geometry, optics, and meteorology; Kant discussed the formation of planetary systems as well as the categories of pure understanding. Ambitious attempts to advance and defend claims about the natural world, without venturing very far into it, waned in popularity only as the need for intricate and demanding experimentation became more evident. Nevertheless, the connections between philosophy and the search for knowledge of nature show the value of informed reflective thought: philosophers with a thirst to acquaint themselves with the best information available to their contemporaries have often found ways of framing a nascent field of inquiry. Philosophical *midwifery*, as I shall call it, is a valuable result of the original urge for systematic knowledge of nature. The service of the midwives is sometimes recognized and appreciated. One of the most effective responses to the complaint that philosophy never makes progress stems from acknowledging philosophy's offspring: "Of course philosophy doesn't make progress! That's because, when philosophers launch a study that plainly makes progress, people don't call it 'philosophy' anymore."

The search for natural knowledge defines one axis along which philosophy has been directed. As that search is undertaken, the form of the question changes. Ancient thinkers wanted to know the fundamental elements out of which the cosmos is built. Two millennia later, it began to become clear that answers to questions like that would require complicated interactions with the natural world to address all sorts of preliminary issues, and that dawning recognition gave rise to a division of labor. From the nineteenth century on, philosophy's role in the search for natural knowledge has been that of an assistant—sometimes, as in recent work identifying causes (Spirtes et al. 2000), of an assistant who is promoted to a full partner. There are places where difficulties arise through conceptual confusion, or where options are limited because some presupposition defines the apparent possibilities—and in these places natural philosophy can still flourish. I'll postpone for the moment any further consideration of this role for philosophy, and of how it can contribute to the enterprise of factual knowledge (the following chapter will offer some examples).

The second axis marked out by Dewey's diagnosis is directed toward identifying value. For Paleolithic people, living together in small bands, as for well-born members of a Greek polis and for citizens of contemporary societies, there were and are issues about what ways of life are worthwhile, what ends are worth pursuing, what rules should govern their interactions, and what institutions they should fashion or maintain. Questions like these arise from the conditions in which people find themselves, and, as those conditions change, we should not expect that the formulations that are most salient or most apt should remain invariant. They are questions that are urgent for all people—or at least for all people who have any chance of directing the course of their lives. They deserve answers that are not only pertinent to the situations in which people find themselves but also are as well-informed as possible about the character of the world in which we live (including what is known about ourselves). Hence Dewey emphasizes the importance of integrating the contributions of various forms of inquiry and of connecting them with our search for what is valuable. As he goes on to remark:

> Man has never had such a varied body of knowledge in his possession before, and probably never before has he been so uncertain and so perplexed as to what his knowledge means, what it points to in action and in consequences. (Dewey 1929/1988, 249)

The evolution of philosophy along the value-oriented axis should respond to the changing circumstances of individual and social life, and also incorporate the best general picture that can be derived from the contributions of the various specialized sciences. Framing that general picture is itself a philosophical problem that emerges along the knowledge axis.

We can now begin to understand how philosophy can continue to be more than a "sentimental indulgence for a few," how it can be a vital part of evolving human culture. Setting aside any further ventures in philosophical midwifery, societies and individuals continue to need an integrated picture of nature that combines the contributions of different areas of inquiry, and different fields of investigation can be assisted by thinkers whose more synthetic perspective can alert them to missed opportunities and provide them with needed clarification. Along the value axis, philosophy can offer an account of morality and of ethical life as evolving practices, a series of such practices that has probably occupied our species for tens of thousands of years (a significant portion of its history), and that has been variously distorted by claims to expertise that are based on alleged religious revelations or on supposed a priori reasoning. Philosophers can seek, as Dewey recommended, methods for advancing these practices, ways to make moral and ethical progress less chancy and bloody, more systematic and complete. The heart of moral philosophy and of ethics consists in identifying ways to improve people's decisions and to reform the institutions framing human conduct. Methodological advice can be garnered from history, fueling attempts to avoid the blind spots of our predecessors, and to diagnose the places in current ethical, social, and political practice where we are similarly unable to see clearly.

Philosophy, so understood, is a synthetic discipline, one that reflects on and responds to the state of inquiry, to the conditions of a variety of human social practices, and to the felt needs of individual people to make sense of the world and their place in it. Philosophers are people whose broad engagement with the condition of their age enables them to facilitate individual reflection and social conversation.

***

I'll attempt to remedy the vagueness of this vision by offering some illustrations with respect to each of the axes along which philosophical discussions should advance. Consider, first, the knowledge-seeking axis. There are, of course, the grand questions that dominate our standard curricula: What is knowledge? Can various forms of skepticism be rebutted? Professional meetings are typically abuzz with spin-offs from these grand questions: Should we opt for internalism or externalism? Is knowledge distinct from belief or a form of belief? We lack firm answers to these questions. That does not seem to matter very much. Inquiry goes on, often delivering valuable results. It is far from evident that it would go even better if especially clever philosophers settled these issues once and for all. Perhaps philosophy's well-known failure to reach answers to its questions stems from its irrelevance: if the issues were truly urgent, wouldn't those who felt their significance demand standards for resolving them?

At times, human inquiry is retarded or even halted because investigators are ignorant or confused about the entities involved in the phenomena they seek to understand. Genetic research was greatly advanced when it was recognized that genes are segments of chromosomes, when it was discovered that paired chromosomes can exchange material, and—dramatically—when scientists recognized DNA as the genetic material (for most organisms; awareness of retroviruses came later). When philosophers grandly ask, "What is knowledge?" or "What makes moral statements true?," it might be well to pose a counter question: "Why do we need to know?" Is it, as in the genetics case, to remove road-blocks to inquiry? Would we be able to gain greater knowledge if we had an answer to the epistemological question? Would settling the issue of the grounds of moral truth assist in moral decision-making? Do the kinds of answers philosophers offer to these questions—and about which they continue their ever more technical debates—enable our knowledge seeking and our moral practices to make progress? For centuries, knowledge of the natural world has grown impressively, even in the absence of "philosophical clarity" about what knowledge is. Perhaps with respect to moral and ethical deliberations, "philosophical clarification" would be welcome—but only if understanding the status of morality led to methods we could follow to make moral progress. I suggest a slogan for a much-needed revolution: No philosophical clarification without methodological edification! *Revolution* is required because so much of contemporary analytic philosophy fails to satisfy that demand.

Some of the questions philosophers continue to pose were once important. In the early seventeenth century, as Aristotelianism crumbled after two millennia of dominance, it was extremely natural to ask how knowledge could be placed on an immoveable foundation. For those who saw the past as an exercise of building on sand, it was important that this should never happen again. Out of their (ultimately unsuccessful) efforts to find firm foundations came many of the questions that dominate philosophy courses today. Yet our predicament is different. We have grown used to the idea that almost everything—or for some of us, everything—is revisable. What issues should arise in our times?

The knowledge axis of philosophy began by seeking to identify the structure of the cosmos. Today it is doubtful that there is any grand structure to be found. As Nancy Cartwright has forcefully argued, we live in a dappled world (Cartwright 1999). The predicament of inquiry is to select questions that are particularly salient for people, given their cognitive capacities and their evolving interests, and then to work to address *those* questions—not to seek some grand "theory of everything." Perhaps some insightful philosophers can help through further midwifery: helping neuroscience in its struggles to tackle hard problems about consciousness, say—although I harbor doubts about whether these topics are tractable in our current situation. Or perhaps philosophers can bring broader perspectives to bear on areas of inquiry where there are protracted controversies and difficulties: in debates about how to square quantum mechanics with the theory of relativity, or in disputes about biological determinants of behavior, for example.

As the division of labor between philosophy and natural science was more firmly instituted in the eighteenth and nineteenth centuries, there was an obvious way to redirect the knowledge seeking of philosophers. The natural scientists would investigate the world, while the philosophers would study the methods of investigation. Provision of canons of evidence, and explication of metascientific concepts—like *theory, law, cause,* and *explanation*—would contribute to philosophical midwifery by demonstrating how nascent sciences might begin to grow. From the efforts of nineteenth-century methodologists, Mill and Peirce, for example, to the attempts of logical positivists, logical empiricists, and contemporary Bayesians, some valuable things have been learned, and we have acquired better tools for the resolution of some scientific controversies. Yet, just as there is no grand theory of nature, so, too, there is no overarching scientific method of any substance. There are the various fields of inquiry with their collection of techniques for assessing hypotheses, techniques passed on to aspiring practitioners in "methodology" courses. If the philosophy of science is to make genuine contributions to the methods used in any of these fields, it must be by delving into the details—as, for example, Clark Glymour and his colleagues do with respect to the discovery and evaluation of causal models from statistical data (Spirtes et al. 2000).

The epistemological questions I've so far considered focus on *individual* knowledge. Yet it should be evident that the principal issues in an age in which so much potential information abounds are *social*. In what directions should inquiry go, if it is to respond to human needs? How is collective knowledge to be certified and its status made clear? How can the body of knowledge we have be organized so it is available for distribution to the people who need it? How are the claims of expertise to be balanced against the claims of democracy? Among others, Alvin Goldman, Nancy Cartwright, and I have begun to consider questions of these types (Goldman 1999; Cartwright 2007; Kitcher 2001, 2011b). I submit that our preliminary efforts are not peripheral investigations that derive from "core epistemology." They are central to a renewal of philosophy at a time when one significant project along the knowledge axis is, in Cartwright's apt phrase, to explore how knowledge can best be adapted "for human use."

***

My earlier discussion of the value axis takes for granted a view of the ethical project that I cannot fully defend here. Like Dewey, I take morality and ethics to be human inventions,[2] although not arbitrary ones. They grow out of our needs and our social condition—they are, if you like, social technologies that respond to the problems of that condition. We have been engaged in moral life for at least fifty thousand years, and for most of that time our moral practices have been worked out in very small groups.

Here is a brief and blunt overview (a more extended account is given in Kitcher 2011a). Our hominid ancestors, like our evolutionary cousins, the chimpanzees, lived in groups mixed by age and sex. They were able to achieve that social state because they had acquired psychological dispositions to respond to their fellows. Like contemporary chimp societies, those hominid groups were constantly in danger of social dissolution because of the limits of the responsiveness: evolution under natural selection has equipped us with psychological dispositions to take the needs of others into account—*sometimes*. Unfortunately, our adaptive equipment allows for many occasions in which we ignore what those around us are attempting to achieve, and our neglect typically provokes social trouble. Unlike our evolutionary relatives, who continue to solve their social problems through time-consuming forms of reconciliation, human beings gained an ability to control some socially disruptive inclinations through self-command. The moral project began when our ancestors deliberated with one another, on terms of (rough) equality among the adult members, all of whom were needed for the survival of the band, and arrived at an agreement on rules that would govern their lives together. They initiated a series of experiments of living—to use Mill's phrase— and we, who come late in that series, have inherited the experimental ideas that were most culturally successful.

We cannot tell whether either natural or cultural selection has any tendency to generate elements of ethical practice that might merit the title of "truth" or "rightness." Yet it is still possible to find a kind of objectivity in our moral codes. The patterns of conduct we praise and the rules we endorse are objective to the extent that they help in overcoming not merely the surface symptoms but the deep cause—the restricted character of our evolved responsiveness to others. Objectivity in that sense enables us to talk of moral progress, not as increasing proximity to independently fixed moral truths, but in terms of problem-solving. The keys we sometimes devise fit some of the locks we need to open. As with other forms of technology, we can understand progress in morality as accumulating solutions to problems. Moral progress has been partial, and vulnerable to reversal, and it occurs significantly less frequently than would be desirable—but it exists. Dewey's hope—which I share—is that an understanding of the character of the moral project (and its offspring, the ethical project) can help us make progressive transitions more frequently, more completely, more reliably, and with more enduring results (Kitcher 2021a).

If anything like this picture is correct, then it bears on the way philosophy should proceed along the value axis. Contemporary meta-ethics, as practiced in the English-speaking world, is full of questions about "reasons" and "knowledge" that an account of ethics as social technology bypasses. Those who use these idioms rarely deploy them to offer methodological advice for ethical inquiry. Their discussions of reasons candidly concede that little can be said about what reasons are. Indeed, we might wonder whether entities appropriately dubbed "reasons" exist. To be sure, people make up their minds by thinking things through, engaging in forms of reason*ing* good or bad. Does that entail the existence of reasons? Although deliberators often describe themselves as doing things for reasons, that hardly clinches the matter. After all, people do things for the sake of those they care about. I suspect very few of them believe in the existence of sakes. It is surely worth asking if contemporary meta-ethics is a Ptolemaic enterprise, resolutely adding epicycles that tend to obfuscate rather than to clarify.

Instead of continuing that venture, we might use the picture I have painted to diagnose the conditions of contemporary ethical practices. They are radically different from those obtaining at early stages of the ethical project. Today, causal involvement with other members of our species takes place on a far vaster scale, and what ethical discussions we have are not undertaken on terms of equality nor with any close connection with many people who might be affected by what we decide. Most importantly, our entire thinking is dominated by the myth that there are experts with final authority to answer ethical questions. Usually these are identified as religious teachers who have access to the will of a being who sets the rules. An alternative and *far* less influential version of the myth takes them to be clever philosophers who have discovered the fundamental principles on which the governance of conduct should rest. Both versions of the myth sometimes fasten on *stable elements* of ethical traditions, principles or ideals that were introduced in a progressive shift and would remain in place under further progressive modifications—we might introduce a notion of ethical truth to mark this feature of them—but instead of presenting these ideals and principles in the vague forms that underlie their stability, religious teachings and philosophical pronouncements, driven by the desire for complete systematization, transform them into universal claims that brook no exception. Better to think in terms of methods for advancing morality, grounded in the idea of engaging with others, and of the contributions of sages, saints, and savants as tools to facilitate that engagement (Kitcher 2021a).

One task for moral practice is to pay attention to the places at which vague moral generalities, the tools we draw from the toolbox, fail to serve us well, either because they are inapplicable to the troubles at hand, or because different tools would generate alternative reforms among which we cannot decide. When this occurs, our best response, I claim, is to facilitate some analogue of inclusive, engaged conversation in a world in which billions of voices are typically lost. Once the myth of final expertise is abandoned, philosophers can only propose. We might seek to emulate the features of the ethical project that dominated its early stages, requiring conversation to engage with the aspirations and needs of others—*all* others, on an equal basis—and that discussion must accord with the best integrated knowledge we have (according to the synthetic philosophical picture generated along the knowledge axis).

One particular task for philosophical inquiry is to attend to the functioning of those roles and institutions that the evolution of the ethical project has generated. Many of the questions people pose about what they should do or about what they should aspire to be are already framed in terms of existing roles and institutions—*caregiver* and *worker*, *property* and *marriage*. Given the picture I have sketched, we should anticipate that roles and institutions were introduced in response to problems that were salient for our ancestors. Through a genealogical investigation, one that traces their original functions, we can prepare the way for exploration of alternatives that are better suited to the problem background of our own times (as, on my interpretation of his work, Michel Foucault attempted to do).

Another task is to address the opportunities for people, individually and collectively, to engage in reflection and conversation about the sense of their lives. Aristotle's brilliant anatomy of the good life proceeds from the circumstances in which elite members of the polis found themselves. We need not only an anatomy that is responsive to the full range of modern human beings but also a physiology that will give, beyond the bare list of possibilities, a sense of how a particular kind of life might be experienced. Dewey recognized the need for a physiology of this sort, and he saw it as proceeding through the interaction between philosophy and the arts:

> As empirical fact, however, the arts, those of converse and the literary arts which are the enhanced continuations of social converse, have been the means by which goods are brought home to human perception. The writings of moralists have been efficacious in this direction upon the whole not in their professed intent as theoretical doctrine, but in as far as they have genially participated in the arts of poetry, fiction, parable and drama. (Dewey 1925/1981, 322)

Work that points to the philosophical significance of literature is not peripheral, but central to a philosophical question that arises in different specific forms in different epochs.

***

Much of what I have said so far needs refinement—and some of that will be provided in later chapters. Yet I don't think my oversimplifications undermine my plea for philosophical redirection. Whether I have the details right, it seems abundantly clear that there are important questions along both axes that philosophy should be addressing, and that much of what is taken to lie at the center of the subject has no obvious bearing on any such question. Appearances might be deceptive. Nevertheless, it is incumbent on philosophers to consider just what, if anything, makes their intended contributions worth having.

Work that genuinely makes a difference is being done at many places in contemporary Anglophone philosophy. Philosophers of the special sciences, not only physics and biology but also psychology, economics, and linguistics, are attending to controversies that bear on the future evolution of the focal field, and sometimes on matters that affect the broader public. Some political philosophers are probing the conditions of modern democracy, considering in particular the issues that arise within multicultural societies. Ventures in normative ethics sometimes take up the particular challenges posed by new technologies or the problems of global poverty. Social epistemology has taken some first, tentative, steps. A growing number of thinkers are engaging with questions of race, gender, and class. Within aesthetics, attention has been paid to connections between art and politics, and some philosophers have followed Stanley Cavell's pioneering work in exploring the philosophical significance of major works of music, drama, and literature (Cavell 1969). In many of these developments, there is a welcome rapprochement between ways of thinking that were too often blocked off from one another by prominent "Stop" signs, marked with one of the two unhelpful labels "Analytic" and "Continental"—as if to travel across the English Channel were to breach a significant philosophical barrier.

The many praiseworthy ventures to which I have just alluded rarely view themselves as part of a common philosophical approach: what, after all, does a critique of rational choice models in economics have to do with an excavation of the moral perspective in the novels of Henry James (Sen 1977; Pippin 2000)? Whatever the degree of shared consciousness, these parts of contemporary Anglophone philosophy realize Dewey's vision, in their attempts to renew philosophy in relation to contemporary life and culture. Dewey's own major works traverse similar terrain, as they range from science to politics, from religion to aesthetics. His descendants may even be seen as exemplifying his account of philosophy as general theory of education, in their serious consideration of the world as the current state of inquiry presents it, in their attempt to provide an integrated vision of that world that can guide the developing individual, in their attention to the meaningful possibilities for that individual, in the shaping of a self that will live in community with others.

What binds these endeavors together is a concern for philosophical questions that matter, rather than a shared method. In setting high standards for precision and clarity, the Anglophone philosophy of the past half century can be valuable for Deweyan practitioners—just as finger-tangling études can be excellent preparation for aspiring pianists. Yet unless one can show that the more abstract questions do contribute to the solution of problems of more general concern, that they are not simply exercises in virtuosity, they should be seen as preludes to philosophy rather than the substance of it. As I said at the beginning, I leave it to those for whom metaphysics and epistemology, philosophy of language and mind, as currently practiced, count as the center of philosophy to respond to the challenge. If that challenge cannot be met, then our current image of philosophy should be turned inside out.

Why does that image matter? What is the point of the metaphilosophical question? I gave one part of the answer already: the common Anglophone conception of philosophy shapes the ways in which practitioners relate to other areas of inquiry and to the problems of everyday human life. A faulty image will mislead the profession of philosophy, and the consequence will be a failure to fulfill the functions with which philosophers are properly charged. My reintroduction of the theme of education suggests the second part of the answer. Graduate programs in philosophy currently train highly intelligent and imaginative young people, whose lives will be dominated for decades by the problems their mentors and colleagues take to be central to the field. We train them well by giving them studies that improve their facility for thinking precisely and rigorously. If, however, the prevailing image of philosophy fails to distinguish the preliminary studies from the genuine work, if it treats what is most important as mere periphery, as a place in which the second-raters slum it, then their education will have failed them. Whether they eventually recognize it or not, they may spend their entire lives knocking a second off the performance of *Multi-Scale 937* or adding an extra trill to *Quadruple Tremolo 41*.

2 | "SO . . . WHO *IS* YOUR AUDIENCE?"

I have a friend, a Shakespearean scholar, whose books are not only acclaimed by his fellow academics but avidly read by many other people. Sometimes, when we meet for a cup of tea or a drink, we talk about our current research topics. I will explain what I am thinking and writing about, and he will listen sympathetically. His own work inclines him to consider how professors might reach a wider public. And, often, he will lean back and ask . . . the question I have quoted in my title: "So . . . who *is* your audience?"

I hate the question. As I've told him, I conceive my writing differently. There are ideas and arguments I want to explore, debates I hope to resolve. My first job is to do justice to the ideas and the reasoning. Once I have that straight, I try to make everything as clear and as accessible as I can. I would like as many people as possible to gain a better understanding of the issues with which I'm concerned. But the articulation of the ideas, the generation of the understanding comes first. The audience will be determined by my ability, first to figure things out, and second to be as clear as possible about what I've done.

What's the Use of Philosophy? Philip Kitcher, Oxford University Press. © Oxford University Press 2023. DOI: 10.1093/oso/9780197657249.003.0002

My friend isn't convinced. He finds this a curious way to think and write. Much as I dislike his question, I've come to think that he has a point. In this chapter, I want to explore it.

***

The trouble is that my title question has a skeptical relative. "Is there *any* audience for the issues that interest you, *any* group of people for whom the ideas and arguments you struggle to clarify are valuable or important?" It's easy to dismiss that form of skepticism, to see yourself as pursuing inquiries that are intrinsically significant, even "fundamental" and "timeless." But I think the skeptical voice deserves a hearing. A century ago, John Dewey worried that many of his fellow philosophers were "socially absent-minded men" pursuing "intellectual busywork." Like him, I don't want philosophy to become "a sentimental indulgence for the few" (Dewey 1916/1980, 338).

Chapter 1 was inspired by a sense of this danger, indeed by a growing conviction that contemporary Anglophone philosophy has lost its audience. I focused concern by comparing today's professional philosophy with its discussions and printed exchanges to a musical culture that had set up competitions to see who could perform études of maximal difficulty in minimal time, and that disparaged those who continued to play the standard (much-loved) repertoire of sonatas and concertos. Here, I proceed differently. I want to look at a particular subdiscipline, one that seems less remote and cloistered than most. Philosophy of science strikes me as a relatively healthy part of philosophy. So I am not in the business of delivering a jeremiad or a lamentation. Instead, I hope to offer a positive answer to the skeptic. But one that, as school reports sometimes suggest, sees "need for improvement."

***

There are three obvious responses to the question "Who is the audience for work in the philosophy of science?" The first proposes that philosophers of science can deliver something of value to philosophy; the second suggests that the practices of the sciences can benefit from philosophical reflection on them; the third views philosophy of science as reaching out beyond the academy and helping the general public to think through issues that are important for individual lives and for the health of human societies. I shall want to consider all three of these possibilities, but, before I do so, it's worth reflecting on the history of the subject and considering how the question would have been answered at various stages.

The prehistory of contemporary philosophy of science begins with the first recorded attempts to reflect on the search for knowledge of the natural world. Ancient thinkers, in many different civilizations, offered their views about the fundamental characteristics of the cosmos. As their different proposals collided, they began to make explicit the ideas about how investigations should be conducted they had tacitly presupposed. Consequently, much of the early exploration of nature mingles substantive hypotheses with claims about how knowledge of the pertinent kinds can be obtained. One aspect of the period in which modern science was born, often characterized as "the scientific revolution," was the increasing separation of substance from method. As experimental practices were developed, and as they were viewed as essential to disciplined inquiry, a division of labor was instituted. Unless philosophers were prepared to go into the laboratory (or, for some sciences, into wild nature) to make rigorous observations, they were no longer expected to pronounce on substantive matters. Their license was restricted to articulating canons of proper inquiry. Work of that type flowered in the writings of those we hail as philosophers, as well as some "philosophical" natural scientists, from the seventeenth to the nineteenth century. It became focused in the early twentieth century in the writings of a group of thinkers who have left an enduring imprint on the way in which philosophy of science is done.

Many of the questions philosophers of science continue to discuss were posed by philosophers displaced in the 1920s and 1930s from Vienna and Berlin—Rudolf Carnap, Hans Reichenbach, Otto Neurath, Herbert Feigl, Carl Gustav Hempel, and others. The Vienna and Berlin circles, influenced by passages in the writings of David Hume and Ernst Mach, looked at the history of philosophy with a suspicious eye—and pledged themselves to doing better. The problem with philosophy, they thought, was not so much that its claims were largely false, but that they failed to possess any clear meaning—or "cognitive significance." Logical positivism, the movement they initiated, sought a criterion of cognitive significance, applicable to all philosophical discussions. It would, they thought, slice away the useless fat, leaving only the healthy substance behind. (Interestingly, although judgments about value were officially carved away, deposited among the fatty leavings, the positivists were not reluctant to adopt a moral stance; they were passionate advocates for political causes, going to great lengths to extricate vulnerable people from the clutches of Nazism, for example.) The body left intact after their surgery, they claimed, consisted of logic (now formalized by Frege, Russell, Hilbert, Wittgenstein, and others whom they admired) and the regimentation of the natural sciences by formal logic. Philosophy's scope was radically reduced. It was to be "the logic of the sciences." The goal of philosophical work, pursued in the various volumes of an ambitious series of monographs, the *Encyclopedia of Unified Science*, was to clarify concepts and expose structures of justification across a wide range of fields of inquiry.

The grand project presupposed a principle, the criterion of cognitive significance. Supposedly there are two kinds of genuinely meaningful statements: some (e.g., the truths of logic and mathematics) are true or false in virtue of the semantic relations among their constituent terms; others go beyond matters of mere meaning to make claims about the world, and these must be verifiable, at least in principle. Regarding the previous sentence (and its kin) as philosophically unsatisfactory, the positivists demanded that the criterion be formulated in approved logical form, so it could be applied to decide difficult cases. Unfortunately, attempts to find a proper formulation proved unsuccessful. Logically kosher versions either debarred important parts of natural science or allowed in the murky sentences against which the positivists railed, and which they dismissed as cognitively insignificant "metaphysics." As it became clear that the difficulties were systematic, the search was abandoned. Logical positivism metamorphosed into logical empiricism. Logical empiricism, born around 1950, then set the agenda for subsequent philosophy of science.

Before we consider that transition, let's ask how the positivists would have identified their audience. They'd have emphasized two out of the three possibilities I mentioned. Not the first, of course. Traditional philosophy is contentless, the pursuit of pseudo-questions (Carnap 1928). That leaves no independent discipline to be enlightened by the philosophy of science. The second possibility, however—addressing scientists—was viewed as especially important. The logical reconstructions of parts of science were offered at a historical stage when the principal foci of philosophical reconstruction were relatively new. For the logical positivists were enthusiastic about physics, and inspired by its early twentieth-century developments. The theory of relativity and quantum mechanics were recent developments, each of them posing difficult scientific questions. Philosophical reconstructions were intended to help clear up some of the scientific puzzles. And they did. Axiomatization enabled practitioners to see the conventionality of choice for the one-way velocity of light and to recognize the equivalence of different formulations of quantum theory.

But this was by no means the only way in which philosophy of science aided the sciences. The *Encyclopedia* was a missionary effort. Through showing the structures of the well-developed sciences (physics!), and reviewing the state of the less-developed ones, the hope was to foster fields of inquiry that were only beginning to find their way. A general picture of how successful science worked would help the psychologists and the anthropologists and the linguists. Moreover, beyond the scope of the second possible answer, there would be illumination for a broader public. Nonscientists would understand the special credentials of the sciences. Their admiration might even translate into efforts at emulation. And, perhaps, the logical reconstructions would prove useful in showing how best to educate the young. Obstacles involved in making some parts of science comprehensible would be overcome.

The transition from logical positivism to logical empiricism preserved many of the previous aims but modified the priorities. Hempel's classic articles on the problems encountered in trying to formulate a precise criterion of cognitive significance conclude by setting a new agenda for the philosophy of science (Hempel 1950, 1951). The old conception of a sharp distinction between the cognitively meaningful and the meaningless gives way to a graded account of the differences among various putatively cognitive ventures. Areas of inquiry differ with respect to their capacities to develop genuine theories, their ability to provide explanations, and the extent to which the claims made by their practitioners are supported by evidence. Hence arise three of the four main enterprises Hempel projects for logical empiricist philosophy of science: to find general accounts of theory, explanation, and confirmation. (The fourth, the explication of simplicity, mostly fell by the wayside.) From 1950 to the present, logical empiricist philosophy of science—the overwhelming majority of *general* philosophy of science—has pursued these tasks, and others that have spun off from them (e.g., an account of the laws of nature, and, most recently, an account of models and their functions).

The priorities shifted in that the focus on theory, explanation, and confirmation became seen as central to the missionary role of aiding the relatively undeveloped areas of inquiry. During the 1950s and 1960s, less emphasis was placed on reconstructing prominent achievements in the special sciences. Philosophy of science seemed to speak mainly to scientists by offering a richer account of the distinctive qualities that had made some groups of natural scientists so spectacularly successful. By doing so, it also offered an image of the sciences to a broader public, one that was occasionally influential in debates and discussions.

Why "occasionally"? Because, for all its orthodoxy among philosophers of science, the logical empiricist picture of axiomatic theories, tied to observational claims through correspondence rules, offering explanations through subsumption under general laws, and confirmed in ways that would be articulated in some still-to-be-completely-developed inductive logic or confirmation theory, was never the most popular account with the general public, with journalists, or even with practicing scientists. That honor fell to the rival approach proposed by Karl Popper (Popper 1934). Popper (another emigré from Vienna) claimed that verifiability was not the key to cognitive significance. What was crucial to meaningfulness was the susceptibility to being shown false. His concept of falsifiability captured the imagination of a broad audience—as witnessed by the frequency with which it has been wheeled out as the hallmark of genuine science, even in famous court decisions.

Moreover, the potential influence of the logical empiricist picture, and also of its Popperian rival, was diminished by the developments of the 1960s and 1970s. Attempts to answer the general questions about the sciences posed by the logical empiricists led a group of philosophers—N. R. Hanson and Stephen Toulmin, as well as Paul Feyerabend and T. S. Kuhn—to consider the historical details of the classic achievements. They replaced the comforting legends of standard presentations with accounts that were far more informed and nuanced. And far more disturbing. Kuhn's monograph (Kuhn 1962) was the final volume in the *Encyclopedia of Unified Science*, and it was well received by many scientists, who saw in the concept of normal science (in which investigators attempt to solve supposedly well-designed puzzles, and in which the world tests *them*, not the framework under which they operate) a far more accurate presentation of their activities than anything previous orthodoxies had been able to offer. Much to Kuhn's regret, "paradigm" slid smoothly into public discussions. To this day, the most prominent general image of science, among outside commentators and scientific researchers, marries pieces of Popper with bits of Kuhn (although neither would be happy to be joined to his bedfellow).

Kuhn's proposals about the difficulties of scientific revolutions, in which one paradigm gives way to another, caused little offense to the scientists who read his monograph. The only people bothered by his references to "faith" and "conversion experiences" were, apparently, philosophers. From the late 1960s on, a principal task of philosophy of science was to show how the historical details might be accommodated without abandoning the conception of the natural sciences as special—as "rational" and as "progressive" (Scheffler 1967; Lakatos 1970; Laudan 1977). The task seemed urgent. Perhaps general attitudes toward science would be corrupted by the awful bogey Kuhn-Feyerabend—a chimera constructed by people (including me) who failed to recognize the important differences between these two thinkers. And it got worse. Feyerabend was very clear that his ideas were different from Kuhn's, and his presentations became ever more flamboyant—and more entertaining (Feyerabend 1978, 1987). Meanwhile, the historicists had inspired other radical developments, including a

sociological parade begun in Edinburgh and extending through
Bath and Paris (Barnes 1977; Collins 1985; Latour 1987). All
the figures enjoying the carnival Kuhn-Feyerabend seemed to
have initiated were taken, by the majority of philosophers of science, to be undermining the authority of science, announcing an
awful relativism that would leave the wider world bereft of proper
guidance. Apparently, our public discussions needed an image of
scientific research that would preserve the proper respect for the
special accomplishments of the natural sciences. Yet, even when
a few professional scientists paid attention, when Paul Gross and
Norman Levitt and Alan Sokal declared the science wars, the
trenches were dug and the shells fell within the walls of the academy (Gross and Levitt 1994; Sokal 1996). A dash of Popper and
a soupçon of Kuhn satisfied the journalists who wrote about science, as well as their readers.

Of course, there were rumblings about the credentials of particular sciences. Particularly evolution. But those who debated
largely adopted an image of science as a special enterprise.
Scientists trotted out their Popper-Kuhn, philosophers tried their
favorite emendations—more complex, definitely arcane, but more
likely consistent. The more general doubts about science (i.e.,
about having "too much of experts") are a later phenomenon, for
which the supposed heretics—Feyerabend or Bruno Latour, say—
should not be held primarily responsible.

Yet, from the 1960s on, there have been other important developments in the field. First is a return to studies of special sciences,
now on a far wider scale. David Hull and Michael Ruse founded
a new philosophy of biology; Merrilee Salmon and Alison Wylie
ventured into archeology; Dan Hausman, Alex Rosenberg, Mary

Morgan, and Nancy Cartwright turned philosophical attention on economics; a host of scholars reinvigorated earlier attempts to study psychology; Patricia Churchland campaigned for neurophilosophy; and, even within physics, *the* science from the classical logical empiricist perspective, attention turned to a far wider range of areas, sometimes centering on the previously understudied uses of experiment, sometimes on areas of physics that had been neglected (thermodynamics and solid-state physics, for instance).[1] Thirty years ago, in an important Presidential address to the Philosophy of Science Association, Arthur Fine suggested that general philosophy of science was dead (Fine 1988). It had given rise to something more profitable, namely philosophical study of the special sciences.

Fine refined the logical empiricist answer to the audience question. Forget about providing a general image of the sciences, either for practicing scientists (who almost certainly don't need it) or for the general public. Philosophy of science earns its keep by fostering the development of the particular sciences. That can occur through helping to clarify particular disputes or to reconstruct parts of a scientific theory so as to aid research. It can also happen through the elaboration of new methods for testing or justifying specific types of hypotheses.

The refinement tacitly absorbs another important evolution in the philosophy of science. A wide-ranging cluster of philosophers in Northern California, the "Stanford school," debunked the old picture of a unified science, in which natural sciences are arranged in pyramidal form, with the most fundamental (physics) as the solid base, and the more specialized sciences (chemistry, biology, neuroscience, and so forth) occupying successively higher layers. As the Stanfordians made clear, the sciences are many (Dupré

1993; Cartwright 1999). Each of them is a complex practice, sharing features in common with other complex practices, and typically elaborating the most general (and banal) methodological theses in ways suited to its particular questions and its particular subject matter. Philosophers can sometimes help in making methodological progress within some scientific domain. They do so not by offering some general advice about methods, but by attending to the specific problems that arise.

Up to this point, philosophy of science could be characterized as epistemology (maybe with a bit of metaphysics thrown in) about a particular kind of subject matter (perhaps knowledge at its most striking). No intersection with other fields of philosophy— ethics, political philosophy, aesthetics, and the like. Why not? As Elliott Sober once reminded me, the absence of values should cause no surprise. For the founding fathers, before they were logical empiricists, were logical positivists—and the positivists denied that value judgments have cognitive content. (However, as I have noted, that didn't inhibit their moral passion in the face of tyranny and oppression.)

The move to a more inclusive philosophy of science began in the 1980s, in the work of some feminist thinkers—particularly Evelyn Fox Keller and Helen Longino (Keller 1985; Longino 1990). Despite the fact that they began with similar questions to those occupying previous philosophers of science—asking what science is and how it is properly done—values started to creep in to the answers they gave. For some of us, they have hung around. But for many philosophers of science—perhaps for most?— the old questions are the right ones. Philosophy of science is epistemology—and maybe metaphysics—of science.

A more inclusive philosophy of science finds room for science (in the singular) as well as the sciences (plural). For science (singular) is a social institution, one that plays a role in social and political life. There are, I suggest, serious value questions, questions about what its role ought to be.

This, however, is to anticipate. My immediate task is to take stock of the story I have told.

＊＊

Contemporary philosophy of science is heir to the history I have—very crudely—rehearsed. And, of course, there are other developments I haven't mentioned, a few of which will occupy me later. Where does that leave us with respect to the audience question? Who belongs in the audience for this kind of philosophy of science?

If you are a refined person, a follower of Fine, you will think that the second possibility is the right one. Philosophy of science should speak to scientists, offering its luminous reconstructions and its methodological advances in specific domains. Perhaps incidentally it should address the general public, explaining (say) why some apparently contentious piece of science is well grounded (think of evolution or climate modeling). Or arguing that some supposed scientifically grounded claim that bears on human lives and human aspirations is actually unwarranted (think of debates about IQ, about the biology of race, about sociobiology, evolutionary psychology, and genetic modification of organisms).

What's the alternative? Some suppose that general philosophy of science isn't dead. Hempel and his successors posed the right questions, and, despite the failure to find fully general answers, philosophy of science should keep plugging away. I am skeptical about cleaving to tradition in this way. The diversity of the sciences—and of human inquiry in general—goes very deep. There are lots of different kinds of theories, many types of explanation-seeking questions, even many species of evidence. To be sure, some, rather thin, general theses can be advanced and defended—and they have already been stated and defended quite enough. When philosophers try for greater precision, along with science-wide scope, accuracy has to give. Generality and accuracy we can manage—so long as we remain vague.

This is by no means to declare that the attempts to wrestle with Hempel's questions are worthless. The partial proposals generated over the past half century and more are not devoid of value. Almost all the juice has been squeezed from the fruit Hempel and other logical empiricists offered. Yet some of the distillations remain valuable for the contexts in which Fine exhorts philosophers to go to work. Consider some of the major proposals for understanding scientific explanation. None of them covers all cases, and none of them provides the final answer to Hempel's question. Yet, in particular contexts, thinking of explanation as subsumption under law (Hempel 1965) or as the ascription of increased probability (Salmon 1971) or as revealing possibilities of intervention (Woodward 2003)—even as unification (Friedman 1974; Kitcher 1981)—can be helpful for clarifying a scientific dispute. Much of the fruitful work in the philosophy of the special sciences depends on applying the curative liquids supplied by the failed efforts to provide a general account.

Moreover, immersion in the special sciences need not be restricted just to one. Those brave enough to explore several branches of science may find them to share methodological problems or conceptual unclarities, so that *general* philosophy of science may spring from addressing a common need. Appeals to causes span several domains of physical science, fields in the biological sciences, as well as psychology, economics, and sociology. Mathematics, often regarded as the hallmark of truly serious science, is deployed to highlight physical (and linguistic) structures and to explain. So arise quests for methods of causal identification and for understanding of mathematical explanations, enterprises in a renewed, post-Hempelian, general philosophy of science (Woodward 2003, 2021; Lange 2017).

Alternatively, you might think my third possible answer has something going for it. Public discussion would go better if there were a well-developed, widely accepted image of the sciences. Perhaps. But most of the time people seem to manage quite well with a vague idea, even with their own blend of Popper and Kuhn. When public distrust wrongly arises (evolution, climate science) or when unsound ideas are greeted with enthusiasm (IQ, evolutionary psychology), proceeding piecemeal and focusing on the special science does just fine.

We have an answer to my title question. It comes with advice. Go and find your special science(s). Write about it (them). Write for (and maybe with) the pertinent scientists. They are your audience.

For all of its attractions, I am not happy with this answer. Let me explain.

***

I began with three possibilities. Only two of them have figured in my cartoon history and the morals drawn from it. When the other one drops out, only Fine's favorite remains.

My first possibility, that philosophy of science might contribute to philosophy, was excluded at the start of my potted history, because, for the logical positivists, there was no independent contentful philosophy for philosophy of science to influence. Of course, along the way to today, that has changed. Indeed, if members of the Vienna and Berlin circles were resurrected among us, they would be appalled by the profusion of incomprehensible speculations.

Long ago, I heard Hempel tell an amusing anecdote about meetings of the Vienna Circle. An early convention was instituted for the discussions. If any of the participants believed what had just been said to lack any cognitive content, he was to shout out "Metaphysics!" Apparently, the shouts were so frequent as to inspire Neurath to propose an amended convention. When some declaration actually possessed cognitive content, he suggested, those who recognized this were to call out "Not Metaphysics!" The tale suggests how those great forefathers would behave at today's philosophical meetings. Those cleaving to the original convention desperately go from room to room, from session to session, exclaiming "Metaphysics!" in ever more agitated tones. Their

Neurathian counterparts are similarly nomadic, but, throughout their days of listening they maintain an increasingly gloomy silence.

In fact, a place for independent philosophy already became apparent after the transition to logical empiricism. The great gray volumes of *Minnesota Studies in the Philosophy of Science*, rich in classics of the field, contained from the beginning modest ventures in the philosophy of mind. Nothing, of course, to the multiplication of modalities, the embrace of essentialism, and the proliferation of supposedly a priori principles that have come to flood philosophical journals.

Despite its epistemological focus, the philosophy of science of the past decades has very little to say to what is often dubbed "mainstream epistemology." And a good thing, too. For philosophy of science has concentrated on the old-fashioned task of assembling tools for sorting out the evidential merits of different claims. It has been, healthily and steadfastly, more interested in promoting inquiry than in tackling strained questions about whether, under particular artificial conditions, a subject can properly be said to know. Where it has wrestled with skepticism, the forms of skepticism addressed have been live options, typically generated from historical or sociological studies of scientific practice, attempts to slay the alleged monsters spawned by Kuhn-Feyerabend.

The metaphysicians of today might, however, learn much from the achievements of philosophers who have studied the special sciences. For anyone trained in the philosophy of biology, many of the pronouncements self-styled metaphysicians make about natural kinds are embarrassing. Given the sophistication of half a century's explorations of causation, from Wesley Salmon, Patrick

Suppes, and Brian Skyrms to Nancy Cartwright, Jim Woodward, and Clark Glymour, listening to many presentations on "the metaphysics of causation" is akin to hearing fingers scraped over a chalkboard. And those steeped in the history of attempts to give a formal account of explanation will see the latest fashions in "the logic of *ground*" as making their painful way into the blind alleys of the past.

Yet, even if philosophy of science has value for general philosophy, you ought to wonder whether the skeptic has been addressed. Finding a scientific or a public audience would appear to settle doubts, although even here we should ask *why* satisfying the needs of these audiences suffices. Serving as a handmaiden to philosophy—to metaphysics, say—only seems to pass the academic buck. An audience of philosophers would be small consolation, if the philosophers served have themselves no significant audience.

Later in this chapter, I shall suggest an answer to this worry: philosophy of science should contribute to a much-needed successor discipline to traditional metaphysics. For the moment, let's consider another part of philosophy, one about which it's much harder to sustain charges of irrelevance. Whether or not you're a fan of contemporary meta-ethics or of the higher reaches of ethical theory, it would be hard to deny that, in the past half-century, philosophical discussions of particular ethical and political questions have made a positive impact on the conditions of human lives (and on the lives of sentient animals). From its inception in 1971, *Philosophy and Public Affairs* has published seminal articles that have shaped public discussions of important ethical and social questions (e.g., Thomson 1971; Singer 1972). As my historical sketch has emphasized, philosophy of science has mostly avoided any questions about values. That is now changing (Douglas 2009).

Specifically, within the past quarter century a number of philosophers have taken up Darwin's suggestion (in the *Descent of Man*) that our ethical life could be understood as a product of our history. The philosophical work has taken two main directions. One, pursued in the pioneering studies of Brian Skyrms, has elaborated formal models for the emergence of norms (Skyrms 1996, 2004). The other, now a dialogue between philosophers and scientists, has attempted to understand the genealogy of morality. The primatologist Frans De Waal, the anthropologist Christopher Boehm, and the psychologist Michael Tomasello have found philosophical fellow travelers, including Patricia Churchland, Kim Sterelny, and me. Perhaps I express the fondness of a partisan when I hope for a sophisticated account of the evolution of ethical life, one that will improve ethical discussions across a range of significant questions.

The first option, then, isn't as unpromising as it might initially have appeared. Philosophy of science might illuminate ethics, and thereby contribute something that would ultimately improve the world in which we live. As Chapter 1 already indicated, attention to evolution might combine with the traditional focus on methodology to reorient ethical discussions away from the currently fashionable meta-ethical concerns with reasons and abstract versions of moral realism, and toward an understanding of moral progress—one that might enable us to have more of it (Kitcher 2021a). Similarly, philosophers engaged with psychology and neuroscience might improve our understanding of moral decision-making (Churchland 2019).

Let's turn now to the second possibility, taking up Fine's thesis that the philosophy of science is the philosophy of the special sciences. Part of this seems importantly correct. Already in the 1980s, the impact of philosophical work on particular areas of science was apparent. Biology was an outstanding example. (As I sometimes used to tell students, philosophers have less effect on physics, since physicists typically don't think they have much to learn from anyone else—except maybe mathematicians; social scientists, by contrast, are sometimes so desperate for any advice that a well-intentioned philosopher might start a trend that spent decades going nowhere; biology is the Goldilocks science, peopled by scientists who have some sense of what they are doing but who are still open to the suggestions of outsiders. I should probably also have recognized psychology as Goldilocks's twin.) Here are some obvious examples of early effects on biology. Fine's colleague David Hull made large differences to systematics, Elliott Sober and William Wimsatt clarified controversies about units of selection, John Beatty addressed long-standing concerns about the concept of fitness. Those early contributions have been extended in a long list, and, as the work of people like Samir Okasha, Peter Godfrey-Smith, and Laura Franklin-Hall shows, the influence on biological practice shows no sign of abating. Moreover, thanks to some recent contributions—those of John Dupré, Ken Waters, and Marco Nathan, for example—the initial emphasis on evolutionary biology has given way to a more inclusive treatment of biological fields.

In fact, my advice to students was wrong. As philosophers of physics began to liberate themselves from the framework of logical empiricism, making use of its tools where studies of scientific practice seemed to show their promise, exchanges of ideas with physicists became more consequential (as in the work of David Albert, Tim Maudlin, and many younger philosophers). Similarly, as philosophers with an interest in the social sciences abandoned the thought of some grand pan-scientific perspective offered by philosophy of science, they have begun to work profitably with scientific colleagues on concrete problems.

A resounding cheer, then, for part of Fine's thesis. However, I think Fine underrated the possibilities of continuing the methodological tradition, begun by the philosopher-scientists (natural philosophers?) of the seventeenth century who revolutionized the physical sciences, continued in the eighteenth and nineteenth centuries (think of Whewell and Herschel, Mill, Darwin, and Peirce), and pursued by the principals who figured in my potted history. As I have already asserted, this tradition strikes me as the healthy enterprise in epistemology (in sharp contrast to the sickly cousin whose spasms are recorded in "mainstream" philosophy journals). Fine perceptively recognized that the disunity of the sciences spelled trouble for the logical empiricist approach to continuing that tradition. What he overlooked, I suggest, was the possibility of different methodological questions, pertinent to particular aspects of scientific practice that were shared by a number of fields.

Two examples stand out. Consider first the revival of causation. Russell famously pronounced the death of the notion of causation. His obituary has turned out to be premature. Many special sciences hunt for causes, and many applied sciences use them. Almost forty years ago, Clark Glymour and Judaea Pearl independently began to explore the possibilities of using directed graphs to frame causal hypotheses from statistical data (Spirtes, Glymour, and Scheines 2000; Pearl 2000). Today, the methodological proposals advanced by Pearl, and, perhaps, even more those articulated by Glymour and the brilliant team he has assembled at Carnegie-Mellon University, are being used across a swath of special sciences. Valuable exercises in methodology have themselves been revived with the resurrection of causality (Woodward 2021). Nevertheless, Fine is partly vindicated. Significant further work in methodology required a different focus (on the problem of finding causal hypotheses), one that was compatible with the disunities found in scientific practice. And, perhaps most importantly, it required a vast amount of dedicated effort on the part of highly talented people.

My second example addresses an even larger lacuna in the logical empiricist approach, one shared with the great tradition out of which it grew. With the conspicuous exception of Peirce, pre-twentieth-century methodologists sought canons of *individual* methodology. They considered how a single investigator should properly adjust belief in light of interactions with nature. Peirce not only recognized that inquiry is a communal affair. He also started to consider the ways in which the efforts of individual researchers might best be distributed if the community is to make epistemic progress—he talked of the "economy of research." Twentieth-century methodology ignored the hint, remaining relentlessly individualistic, until—interestingly—Kuhn's celebrated monograph highlighted the scientific community and recognized the possibility of reasonable cognitive variation within it.

Inspired by this idea, as well as by David Hull's attention to social processes in scientific inquiry (and only belatedly discovering that Peirce had been there before me), I made some clunky attempts at formal models of community inquiry. Those efforts have been advanced by Michael Strevens, and more recently by younger scholars who have deployed far more sophisticated mathematical tools (Kevin Zollman and Cailin O'Connor are two prominent examples). To cite just one example, unfamiliar to most philosophers, the senior scholar Rainer Hegselmann, formerly of the University of Bayreuth, has developed extraordinarily sophisticated models of the flow of information in scientific networks; a quick visit to Google Scholar will reveal just how unusually influential Hegselmann's principal article (Hegselmann and Krause 2002) has been.

As in the case of methods for identifying causes, a change of focus opens the way for methodological investigations that cut across scientific disciplines. I am surely partial, but, despite my great admiration for the achievements of Pearl, Glymour, and their associates, I view social methodology, formal and informal, as the great area for epistemology today. Detailed studies of scientific practice, carried out by philosophers, historians, and sociologists, have revealed many aspects of communal inquiry. That invites philosophical reflection. Are the conventions and norms governing interactions within scientific communities conducive to the progress of inquiry? Do the conventions on publication and rewards for discovery interfere with the sharing of scientific information? How much disagreement should scientific communities tolerate? Questions of this sort are obviously difficult, but answers would be profoundly relevant to the practice of the sciences. We should amend a famous line by Marx: The philosophers have ignored the social structure of science. The point, however, is to change it.

Thus, I agree with Fine that scientists are an important audience for the philosopher of science. But I want to expand the range of topics beyond those emphasized in his prophetic address.

***

And I also want to make a case for the third possible audience. Indeed, at this particular moment in human history, the need to present scientific issues clearly to people who are not scientists seems to me the most crucial task of all. The rest of this chapter will be devoted to explaining and defending that view, idiosyncratic as it may initially appear.

We live at a time when many decisions profoundly affecting human lives turn on the details of the sciences, sometimes with respect to matters on which a community of scientists agree, sometimes on topics about which there is lively debate. When citizens of affluent democracies have misguided views about what policies (and which candidates) will advance their goals, their choices at the ballot box can run directly contrary to their interests. Ironically, the act through which democracy is often taken to express its commitment to individual freedom then undermines that freedom. Where misinformation is rife, democracy starts to collapse.

Hence, advancing the knowledge of citizens is an important task. If philosophers writing for the general public were able to make their readers more likely to understand and accept the consensus views of an expert community—think of climate change—that would be a valuable achievement. By the same token, if they were able to unmask inadequately supported claims about genetic determinism—think of controversies about the inevitable limitations of women and racial minorities—they would have contributed to the general good. To write about socially consequential parts of science for a nonacademic audience is to perform a public service. Succeeding with that audience delivers the most obvious answer to the skeptical question.

But why would this be a project for philosophers of science? Wouldn't scientific practitioners be much better at doing it? The short answer is that recent history shows how a combination of efforts from writers with different backgrounds and abilities has often proved profitable. In the original controversies about the fixity of IQ, the geneticist Richard Lewontin played an important role—but so did Ned Block and Gerald Dworkin. In debates about the credentials of evolution, Niles Eldredge, Stephen Jay Gould, Ken Miller, and Douglas Futuyma had an important impact— as did Michael Ruse, Barbara Forrest, and Robert Pennock. Lewontin, Leon Kamin, and Stephen Rose offered a powerful case for the speculative nature of human sociobiology—but I like to believe that John Dupré and I have added something. (Not apparently enough, however, to prevent the old fallacies from pervading many prominent efforts at evolutionary psychology. Perhaps my own critiques would have had more lasting impact if they had been delivered less pugnaciously?) With respect to climate change, despite the best efforts of James Hansen, Michael Mann, Naomi Oreskes, and others, even the most basic thesis—the claim that anthropogenic climate change is real—remains disputed. Here, input from philosophers has been largely focused on methodological issues about modeling, recapitulating the view of philosophy of science as focused on epistemology. More is needed, however. Demands for climate action are currently entangled in a cluster of debates in which science, economics, political theory, and hard questions about values all figure. Philosophy of science ought to offer a more comprehensive analysis in which all the difficult topics are addressed (Evelyn Keller and I have made a first attempt at this; Kitcher and Keller 2017).

I don't think there is any great mystery about why philosophers have been able to make contributions in the areas I've cited. To be sure, recent decades have witnessed the emergence of an important scientific genre. Eminent scientists have written superb books and articles for a wide audience. Happily, they have been applauded for doing so. It is no longer true, as it was forty years ago, that scientific colleagues would utter "popularizer" with a sneer. Yet, despite the excellence of many presentations of major scientific ideas by experts in the pertinent fields, philosophers of science have brought a special set of skills to their own—typically complementary—expositions. Trained to think hard about evidential relations, they have sometimes found ways of showing more clearly than their expert scientific colleagues how justification works or where exactly it is lacking. The best account I know of the interpretive difficulties posed by quantum mechanics was written by a philosopher, albeit one with a PhD in physics (Albert 1992). Logical empiricists, of course, believed that their philosophical reconstructions of parts of science would be especially illuminating. But their belief in the "logic of the sciences" was held by the idea of a very particular form in which parts of science should be reconstructed. Eighty years on, philosophers of science take a far more diverse set of approaches to laying bare the conceptual structures and evidential relations, although they continue to deploy tools forged by predecessors who sought general answers to Hempel's three big questions.

Since I have spent significant periods of my life on projects of the kind just described, it is hardly surprising that I should see this kind of writing as a major part of the answer to my Shakespearean friend's question (Kitcher 1982, 1985, 1996, 2007). But I want to close this case study by suggesting that, important though it may be, it is by no means the sole way in which philosophy of science should address the general public. In recent years I've come to view a different, more general, philosophical task as more important still.

***

As I remarked earlier, feminist scholars who attended to the practices of science—and I see Evelyn Keller and Helen Longino as pioneers—taught us to see science, the institution, in relation to human lives and to our sociopolitical condition. I was slow to take the lesson. But my involvement with the Human Genome Project brought home to me what Keller and Longino had so clearly seen—the importance of raising ethical and political questions not only about the practices of the different sciences but about science as an institution.

In retrospect, the sheer weirdness of the fact that, for decades, philosophy of science has been "all epistemology and metaphysics, all the time" seems blindingly obvious. Even when scholars, influenced by Kuhn, started to think about scientific communities as heterogeneous, and not as large individuals with a single mind, social studies of science were dominated by issues about truth and knowledge. Much of the disagreement between philosophers of science and sociologists of science can probably be explained by seeing the socially oriented scholars as forced to pursue questions about values by other means. Were their flirtations with relativism simply a hangover from the positivist assumption that reason breaks down when value judgments enter the discussion?

Thanks to Heather Douglas, Torsten Wilholt, and others, the limitations of the value-free ideal are now recognized (Douglas 2009; Wilholt 2009). Yet, in many corners of philosophy of science, the old questions—and often the old, inadequate answers—remain popular. To be sure, new directions are being pursued in centers that explore the connections among scientific research, public policy, and the quality of human lives. Important work is being done at Western University in Canada, and at many places in Europe: Bielefeld and Hannover, Munich, Rotterdam, Durham, and—definitely not least—at Exeter. Under John Dupré's leadership, Exeter's Center for studying the social implications of the genome project, Egenis, has flowered into a model for socially relevant thinking about science.

To my mind, we need much more ethically and politically informed philosophy of science. Many general questions about the proper role of science in democratic societies and with respect to human lives have yet to be addressed adequately. There are specific ethical issues about many kinds of research, especially in the biological and the human sciences. As Nancy Cartwright and her collaborators have demonstrated, methodological and value-theoretic questions intertwine in considering the evidential bases of policies with large human impact (Munro et al. 2017). Perhaps most urgent of all is the tangle of problems—epistemological, ethical, economic, technological, social, and political—that are generated by anthropogenic climate change. I applaud the fact that some philosophers of science have begun to study the simulations used by climate modelers (Lloyd and Winsberg 2018; Parker 2020; Winsberg 2018). But, to repeat, a far wider philosophical focus is needed.

Skeptics about the possibility of important contributions to such difficult issues might take heart from another philosophical example. As I noted in the previous chapter, a series of articles about the concept of race, some by scientifically informed philosophers, has transformed understanding of that concept. It has helped to influence public debates. Since the earliest such articles, written in the 1990s, the progress has been extraordinary.

***

Finally, I also want to outline a philosophical task beyond these particular endeavors, an enterprise I take to be almost unappreciated. Start with a question akin to the one with which I began. Why do we continue to read the great philosophers of the past? Not, I think, simply because contemporary thinkers enjoy working through the intricacies of the reasonings of their predecessors. Sometimes, it must be admitted, there are deeply disappointing moments—the Cartesian circle, Mill's attempt to prove the principle of utilitarianism, Kant's second analogy (maybe P. F. Strawson was right—it was "a non-sequitur of numbing grossness"?). The real achievements of the Western philosophical tradition lie in the magnificent syntheses provided by thinkers who reflected widely on the achievements of the past and the conditions of life as they encountered it. Philosophy at its greatest is *synthetic*. It doesn't work beside the various areas of inquiry and culture and practice. Instead, it works between and among them. As Dewey puts the point, it tries to offer the *meanings* of what human beings have come to know. In that consists the successor discipline we need to replace the metaphysics of the past.

In a highly complex world, the project of offering an illuminating synthesis of every significant aspect may be too ambitious for any individual thinker. Philosophers are often disinclined to collaborate, but perhaps it is worth considering a more cooperative future. An obvious alternative would be to focus on a particular facet of the world as we find it. Philosophy of science would contribute a general picture of the sciences and of science as an important institution in human societies.

For all their faults, logical positivism and logical empiricism undertook part of that task. So, too, did Popper and Kuhn. Their greater influence may stem from their willingness to connect, from time to time, with social and political issues. Today, perhaps because we recognize the heterogeneity of scientific practices, the philosophy of science has not yet offered any convincing substitute. Ironically, though, the best versions we have emerge in the writings of prominent "disunity theorists"—Longino, Cartwright, Dupré, Ian Hacking, Hasok Chang, and Michela Massimi.

So I offer a threefold answer to my original question. The audience for philosophy of science *should* include philosophers, scientists, and thoughtful members of the public (the supposed, possibly mythical, "educated general reader"). If, as a matter of fact, any of these groups—*especially* the last—is playing truant, it's part of our responsibility to try to bring them back. Occasionally, a philosopher can speak to all three audiences at once—as Daniel Dennett has shown for almost three decades, and as Peter Godfrey-Smith has done in his recent books (books with an unusually wide readership) exploring the character of experience across many species (Godfrey-Smith 2016, 2020).

It's time for the end-of-term report card. Progress has been made in recent years. Philosophers of science are more attentive to the practices of the sciences than they were several decades ago. They sometimes help to clarify issues with which their scientific colleagues are wrestling. Many have abandoned the search for general answers to questions about "the nature of explanation" or "the structure of scientific theories" or "the character of confirming evidence." The entanglement of scientific work with values has begun to be taken seriously.

Yet there is plenty of room for improvement. Efforts to tackle the questions on Hempel's agenda continue to yield vastly diminished returns (to the extent that they yield anything at all). With depressing frequency, the immersion in a particular piece of scientific work generates reportage, as the author's fascination with the details of the study loses sight of any philosophical point, or, indeed, any discernible message for anyone who doesn't share the writer's obsession. Consideration of "science and values" is uninformed by broader discussions of values. No large synthetic vision is on offer to replace the conceptions presented to the public in the past. Far too many talks, too many articles, too many books still provoke my Shakespearean friend's uncomfortable question.

Some philosophers of science have reflected on that question and know what their own answer to it would be. Too many, I fear, have not.

3 | PATHOLOGY REPORT

A wareness of trouble begins, for most of us, with a sense of discomfort. Something has gone wrong, but, until we have consulted people more expert than ourselves, we are in the dark about what it is. We need a diagnosis—a pathology report.

In the two previous chapters, I have tried, impressionistically, to arouse discomfort, by contrasting the state of much contemporary Anglophone philosophy with foils that appear much healthier. The present discussion attempts to pinpoint causes of trouble. I shall identify six problematic features found in the writings of today's professional philosophers—six diseases of today's philosophical practice. Some people are infected as undergraduates; others succumb during their graduate training; a few are eventually cured; but, for the majority, at least one type of malady is, I fear, a permanent condition.

As with some bodily diseases, the pathologies arise out of hyperfunctionality. Just as the body can become sick when a process normally required for good health goes into overdrive—think of the production of thyroid—so, too, a healthy philosophical impulse, pursued with a monomaniacal fetishism, can generate a diseased, even moribund, philosophical practice.

Diagnosticians are in the business of deciding "normal ranges." That is typically difficult, requiring attention to a variety of subjects and a variety of ambient conditions. First attempts are unlikely to be correct. They aim simply to initiate a process through which the differentiation of pathology from normal functioning can be successfully refined.

So my pathology report is preliminary. It tries to isolate a few intellectual virtues that, when acclaimed to the point of obsession, become vices. When that occurs, I contend, philosophy turns inward, becoming the "sentimental indulgence for the few" that Dewey feared and losing its audience. Where exactly that occurs, and the extent to which it is prevalent in contemporary professional philosophy, are matters for discussion. Some people will surely contest particular examples I use. Reasonably enough, the bounds of functionality should be debated. I hope, however, for agreement on the reality of the diseases. For that would be enough to start the self-questioning on which philosophy, throughout its history, has rightly prided itself.

***

In a famous article, Charles Sanders Peirce reflected on how our ideas can be made clear (Peirce 1878/1974). He began from a simple, but important, point. Many people know the meanings of the words they use, in the sense of being able to provide the dictionary definition, without much facility in applying those words to the world they experience. Peirce thought this was the case with the idea of truth, and he offered a famous (and controversial) exposition of the concept. I'll offer a different and easier example. "Democracy" is a word in frequent employment these days, as political commentators and those who listen to them wonder if democracy is dying, whether it still exists in particular parts of the world, and what is responsible for its decline. All of us, if asked, would produce a definition—probably by identifying democracy with government by the people. Yet the commentators, and their followers, disagree quite radically in their judgments about the current state of political life. Not all of them can be correct. Indeed, it seems reasonable to wonder if *anyone* is correct.

Peirce's own response to predicaments of this kind was to supplement the definition with something explicitly designed to help people use the pertinent concept in dealing with their experiences. The exposition is intended to make them able to use the concept smoothly in the contexts where they need, or want, to employ it. In principle, different expositions might be valuable for different classes of contexts. The point is to get the jobs done, to enable people to overcome the obstacles they face in deploying ideas. His essay presupposes a pragmatic standard, one pervading several of his early articles. You scratch only where it itches. "Let us not pretend to doubt in philosophy what we do not doubt in our hearts" (Peirce 1868/1974, 157). Our ideas are tools. We need to be able to use them for the tasks arising for us.

Logical positivism, equally concerned with clarification, proceeded differently. The inability of the definition to enable those who know it to apply the concept testifies to the inadequacy of what is taken as a definition. Hence arises an alternative to Peirce's strategy. Instead of a supplement to the definition, what is needed is a replacement for it. The user's predicament demonstrates the deficiency, typically in some lack of clarity in the defining formula. What's needed, then, is to clarify the vague language occurring in the commonly accepted definition. For the positivists, this meant using a privileged language, one whose terms could be understood without definition. Basic logical terms and terms whose meanings can be grasped through observation uniquely enjoy the privilege. Hence satisfactory definition (or "explication") must eventually be presented using only observational vocabulary and the language of logic.

Contemporary "analytic" philosophy, dominant in the English-speaking world, retains part of the positivist program. Philosophy's central task is seen as one of providing analyses of concepts, analyses exact enough to make the concept completely clear. The positivist insistence on reduction to terms of a privileged language is, however, relaxed. It is replaced by a test: the analysis must decide whether or not the concept applies in any possible case.

That test is more stringent than Peirce's pragmatic attitude. Instead of crafting a tool suited to the particular jobs awaiting attention, analytic philosophy yearns for an all-purpose instrument. If that proves unattainable, the appropriate fallback position is to distinguish a number of concepts capable collectively of applying in all cases (including not only all that actually arise, but all that could occur). At just this point, the commendable demand for clarity goes into overdrive. The result is the *fetish of complete clarity*—an analysis that would leave no potential instance undecidable.

Hence the familiar style of many articles in the most prestigious philosophy journals, a style that sometimes amuses, and sometimes appalls, any nonprofessional reader who may take a look. An analysis of a concept—perhaps it's *knowledge*, perhaps it's *moral responsibility*, perhaps it's *if x were to be the case, then y would be the case* (the counterfactual conditional)—is proposed. The author demonstrates the ability of the favored analysis to yield satisfactory results in a significant range of circumstances. A few journal issues later comes a reply: the proposed analysis doesn't deliver the correct answer for certain other cases (I'll postpone until later how judgments about the "correct" answer are made). The critique invites attempts at repair, as well as new styles of analysis. Through a whole sequence of journal issues—over the years, perhaps even over decades—versions compete, counterexamples multiply, and the cases to which the concept is to be applied become ever more outré. Along the way, perhaps, some reflective author discerns two types of approaches in the "literature," rival perspectives on the analytic problem. The recognition inspires a further debate about the relative merits of these perspectives. And so it goes.

Typically, though not always, the enterprise begins with a live problem. Clarifying the concept of democracy, or of moral responsibility, would serve important practical purposes. That's because, considering the state of a nation or the conduct of a person, questions about the application of those concepts cannot be settled with the definitional tools at hand. When that occurs, analytic work is genuinely valuable. The fetish of complete clarity, however, drives philosophers to keep trading other-worldly scenarios and analyses putatively adequate to them long after the difficulties provoking the original analytic quest have been overcome. No further itch remains. But the fetishists keep scratching. Moreover, even when the original analytic project is (temporarily) suspended, it may enjoy a ghostly continuation in debates about the distinctions that have been drawn as a result of prior exercises of the fetish. The zeal for analyzing "S knows that p" abates, but controversies about the merits of externalism and internalism and contextualism thrash on. And on.

Peirce's emphasis on crafting instruments to advance our actual purposes is salutary. It is echoed in one feature of the positivist program, the turn from definitions of concepts as people—"ordinarily"—use them, to explications that reshape the old concept to fashion a better tool, one more adapted to the actual employments envisaged for it. When philosophers no longer ask after the point of a concept, they not only devote themselves to exploring bizarre fantasies of no practical significance; they also lose sight of possibilities of conceptual reform. We need to adjust our concepts, to re-engineer them, when they do not help in the work for which they are needed— in *our* world for people with *our* purposes. We lack world enough and time to fix them to apply to any circumstances creative minds can imagine and with respect to any conceivable ends. Engaging in so ambitious a venture is a foolish luxury. Its result is a sequence of performances, game-playing at whose virtuosity the well-socialized reader may marvel, while outsiders are impressed (depressed?) by the pointlessness of the enterprise. To the extent that onlookers remain sympathetic, they can only feel sad that people of such evident intelligence waste their lives on such trivial disputes.

***

The second pathology is related to the first. It may be an extension of the fetish of complete clarity, or it may be divorced from the demand to settle all possible cases. The fetish of formalization modifies the positivist requirement to use a privileged language in definition or explication. The idea of formal logic as a clarifying instrument is retained. Proposals about a privileged set of non-logical terms are abandoned.

Sometimes formalization, the use of an artificial quasi-mathematical language, is strikingly helpful in advancing inquiry. Hidden presuppositions are exposed. That occurred in the late nineteenth century, in Hilbert's classic axiomatization of Euclidean geometry. It goes on today in any number of scientific contexts—for example, in the modeling ventures of physicists, biologists, and economists. Moreover, a formal treatment can deliver surprising results—as when Gödel demonstrated the impossibility of Hilbert's attempt to prove (using finitary means) the consistency of arithmetic. Or it can shed light on apparently puzzling phenomena, as in Thomas Schelling's elegant demonstration of how racial segregation can arise in the absence of any strong prejudice, or in George Akerlof's explanation of the breakdown of an unregulated market in used cars (Schelling 1978; Akerlof 1984).

These benefits can accrue within philosophy, too. Thanks to the formal work of David Lewis and Robert Stalnaker (Lewis 1973; Stalnaker 1968), subtle difficulties in counterfactual reasoning have been uncovered. The embryonic field of formal social epistemology has already disclosed some surprising results about the factors that promote or retard the collective search for knowledge. And, of course, Gödel's famous result about the incompleteness of formal systems of arithmetic sits on the borderline between mathematics and philosophy.

Formal methods can be powerful tools in the quest to think clearly about significant questions. Those who do the hard work of developing new and fruitful styles of formalization deserve sustained applause—it often requires years of dedicated efforts. Hence my admiration for the work of Pearl and for that of Glymour and his coauthors. They have transformed the ways in which the scientists who work with statistical data (researchers in a wide range of fields) hunt for causes.

Yet it is possible to make a fetish of formalism, to demand formalization when it would not yield any further fruits, to insist on introducing a quasi-mathematical apparatus when an informal or semiformal account is already clear enough, or is, at least, an advance on the prior situation. Almost all (perhaps even all?) philosophers have had the experience of struggling through a paper bristling with symbols only to find, at the end, a disappointingly banal conclusion, supported by reasoning that could have been characterized in far simpler terms. Sometimes it almost seems as though the author is deterring potential critics, that the purpose of the notation is to warn off those who might attack—as if the philosopher were mimicking those butterflies whose defense consists in mimicking unpalatable relatives.

C. G. Hempel was no opponent of formal methods. Yet he acknowledged the limits of the quest for formalization and was careful to warn graduate students against overdoing it. As he pithily remarked, we gain no greater clarity by rewriting "A man crossed a road" as

$$(\exists x)(\exists y)(Mx \ \& \ Ry \ \& \ Cxy)$$

and even less by rewriting "The man crossed the road" as

$$(\exists x)(\exists y)((z)(Mz \equiv z = x) \ \& \ (w)(Rw \equiv w = y) \ \& \ Cxy)$$

Perhaps Hempel's cautions descended from his own seminal work on scientific explanation. After his efforts to construct a formal account of explanation had encountered repeated difficulties, he turned to an extensive and thorough attempt to articulate his guiding idea, using a mixture of semiformal devices, carefully chosen examples, and lucid definitions offered in ordinary language (Hempel 1965).

Philosophers of science working on explanation have largely followed Hempel's example, introducing some pieces of formal machinery at points where they seem helpful, and resorting to informal characterizations where adequate symbolization runs out. What advances in understanding have been achieved by thinking of explanation as subsumption under laws, or identifying causes, or as answering why-questions, or as achieved through unification have largely come from the authors' initial presentations. Later discussions, bent on "remedying the unclarities" of those presentations by introducing more formalism have typically yielded diminishing returns. The fetishism of formal tools provokes more scratching where there is no itch. (I have surely succumbed to the fetish at times in my own writings, both in some of my attempts to characterize explanation and in at least parts of the last chapter of *The Advancement of Science* [Kitcher 1993], to mention just two evident instances.)

The study of confirmation has also benefited from formal methods. The idea that people have degrees of belief—perhaps related to their willingness to bet—is a powerful one. When coupled to thinking of degrees of belief as rightly governed by probability theory, it yields useful advice about *some* situations in which ordinary people, as well as researchers, must react to new evidence. A classic example: You learn that you have tested positive for some rare but devastating disease; knowing that the false-positive rate is low (only 2%), you are in despair. Your spirits are lifted by a friend, a philosopher who espouses a Bayesian approach to confirmation. She points out to you that you are neglecting the base rate: only one person in a million has the disease. After she lays out the arithmetic for you, you discover that your rational degree of belief that you have the disease is (roughly) simply one in five thousand.

Ambitious confirmation theorists take this dynamic to be at work when inquiry is properly conducted. That suggestion proves helpful when statistics are available (as in the disease example). In many decision situations, however, there are no helpful figures to guide those attempting to find their way forward. To apply the Bayesian machinery, you need two kinds of probabilities that are often elusive: the prior probability of any hypothesis under consideration, and the probability of the evidence if the hypothesis were false. All too frequently, any choice of numbers for these probabilities would be guesswork. Sometimes, to be sure, decision-making can be advanced by relaxing the demand for precise assignments; Isaac Levi's work on inexact probabilities has inspired some useful refinements, both within the orthodox Bayesian tradition and outside it (Levi 1974). So, too, the understanding of how to adjust our degrees of belief to the evidence is advanced by results showing how and when people who begin with different assignments of probabilities will converge—in the long run; despite Keynes's reminder that "in the long run we are all dead," convergence theorems might guide an inquiry to finding evidence that would accelerate consensus.

Nevertheless, all too many important scientific decisions, past and present, could not and cannot be made in the way formal theorists envisage. Consider the prediction that, by 2070, over a billion people will be forced to leave their homes because increases in local temperatures will make those places uninhabitable. Despite a vast amount of evidence about the changing climate, nobody has a formal calculus for assigning a probability to that hypothesis. The best those who deliberate about the issue—like the Intergovernmental Panel on Climate Change (IPCC)—can do is to rely on the informal judgments of a very wide population of experts (who make their own best guesses). Fetishistic formalization aims to drive out judgment. Often, however, the judgment of the experienced is the best we have. Reasonableness outruns the kind of rationality that demands algorithms and is never satisfied without calculations.

Once this point is appreciated, it is possible to see how a valuable philosophical program can degenerate into insignificance, pressing for formalization when playing with the existing tools will only yield tiny returns, if any at all. Although the philosophy of science is a relatively healthy subdiscipline, its zest for formalization *über alles* sometimes needs to be restrained.

Formalistic fetishism is more evident in other parts of philosophy. Sometimes, to be sure, using some existing formal language enables an author to avoid ambiguity in the presentation of some putative principle. All too often, however, the introduction of the notation seems to be designed to add extra importance to some relatively straightforward idea (prestige inflation) or to provide armor against the missiles expected from critics (objection deterrence). Both motivations can inspire an author to devise an entirely novel notation when standard formal languages seem insufficient. Here, the formalism fetish opposes the fetishism for complete clarity. Indeed, the thesis that formalization always brings clarification should always be treated with suspicion. Dedicated readers must usually work hard to penetrate an initially opaque symbolism. As they trudge through the pages, they may wonder whether the effort is worth it. Perhaps they are kept going by their recognition that journal editors will hold their own submissions to the standards set by previous "contributions to the literature"—and thus require them to be familiar with the contents of this article (and many others, no doubt).

Some new formalisms, of course, do earn their keep. Since the pioneering efforts of Frege, Russell, Hilbert, and Gödel, philosophers have had to become acquainted at least with first-order logic. Subsequent decades have witnessed developments in modal logics, applications of Boolean algebra and probability theory, the Lewis-Stalnaker formalisms for counterfactuals, and many other less widely used formalisms, each of which has done honest work. Recognizing and appreciating these developments should not inspire a thoughtless license to couch banal thoughts in an impressive and idiosyncratic idiom or controversial ones in an opaque and idiosyncratic notation.

Nor should those who love formalism neglect two lessons from history. First, whatever his own motivations for inventing the *Begriffsschrift*, Frege's pioneering work in formal logic gained recognition only when it was recognized as addressing the mathematical problems of the age—as helping to resolve the ambiguities of some allegedly complete proofs, focusing existing disputes about the construction of the real numbers, facilitating the kinds of studies envisaged in Felix Klein's *Erlanger Programm*—and calling forth the paradoxes of naïve set theory. Frege's work was initially ignored because his contemporaries, mathematicians as well as philosophers, saw it as much ado about remarkably little. They were wrong—as I may be wrong about some of the ventures that I regard as pointless exercises. Yet the aspiring formalist should always pose the question: For just what kind of clarificatory work is this notation needed?

The second lesson comes from the career of theories of scientific explanation. Sometimes a little formalism is all that is needed. Today, especially in analytic metaphysics, the urge to clarify drives new programs of formalization. It is entirely reasonable to scrutinize claims that some aspects of the world are "grounded" in others. Equally reasonable to appreciate a kinship with the concept of explanation: it seems, at least initially, that x is grounded in y just in case we would explain x by appealing to y. If that equivalence is even in the ballpark of the truth, it might be advisable to reflect on the reasons for which, in a number of alternative traditions, the idea of a complete formal theory of explanation was abandoned. That has implications for those who seek "the logic of *ground*."

So, too, for analytic metaphysics generally, for parts of analytic epistemology, and even for some segments of analytic meta-ethics. Practitioners should always ask: Am I in the business of formalizing "The man crossed the road"?

***

Up to this point, I have left unaddressed the question of how philosophers should decide whether a proposed analysis, formal or informal, passes muster. That is something every well-brought-up twenty-first-century graduate student knows. You use "cases," hypothetical scenarios, to test (or prompt) "intuitions" about them. You give them names—"Fat man on bridge," "Visiting sick friend," or whatever. Let's call this one: "Philosopher deciding."

Philosopher Deciding

Derek is a philosopher, trying to decide whether a particular ethical principle is correct. He considers a wide variety of cases to which the principle might be applied. Finding that, in some of them, his intuition is that it holds, while, in a few of them, his intuition tells him that it does not, he modifies the principle. The new version is—intuitively—satisfied in all the cases. But, pressing further, he invents new cases in which his revised principle breaks down (as he discovers through consulting his intuition). Accordingly, he revises the principle again and repeats the procedure. After a number of iterations, he is content. The principle at which he has now arrived is—intuitively—completely successful. He judges it to be correct. Is Derek's final judgment justified?

What are your intuitions about this case?

As most philosophers will appreciate, I have named the protagonist for the most brilliant and astute artist of the genre, a philosopher who made seminal contributions in a number of philosophical fields, most notably (in my, perhaps nonmainstream, view) in thinking about potential obligations to restrain the growth of the human population (Parfit 1984, Part IV). Derek Parfit deployed this method with enormous skill and sophistication—and sometimes very convincingly (in parts of Parfit 2011). Nevertheless, I want to ask: when, if ever, is this a good approach to deciding philosophical questions?

A rough version of my preferred answer: when, using the capacities we have acquired during our education and socialization, we can think ourselves into the situation envisaged. On occasion, thanks to our past development, it's easy to imagine being in the situation described—or to imagine observing someone else in that situation—and to ask what we would be moved to do (or, in the third-person case, how we would judge the protagonist's action). Long ago, in a famous, and rightly influential article, Peter Singer introduced a compelling example (Singer 1972).

Drowning Child

You are well-dressed for a social event. On your way to it, you pass a pond, and observe a child in the water. The child is obviously struggling, and although the pond is not very deep, will drown unless someone intervenes. You are the only person in the vicinity. To wade into the water would make your clothes wet and muddy, so that you would be inappropriately clad for the occasion to which you are headed. What should you do?

Like Singer, like every other philosopher I know, like all the undergraduates to whom I have ever told some version of this story, I take the answer to be obvious. You should plunge in and rescue the child. Simply walking on and arriving unsullied at the party would be monstrously immoral. (To recognize the case as successful in generating consensus about it is not, though, to endorse Singer's provocative conclusions about the obligations of the relatively well-off. As a lengthy debate has made clear, there are serious questions concerning the analogy between the child in the pool and the significant fraction of the human population who suffer from extreme poverty.)

So far, so good. Let's now proceed to a case, equally famous, introduced in Foot (1967), on which many philosophers would agree, but, as I have discovered, which often fails to elicit the same confident reaction.

Runaway Trolley: Trackside View

As you approach some trolley tracks, you observe, to your horror, that five people have been strapped to the rails. Worse, a trolley is hurtling toward them at high speed. In a few moments it will collide with these unlucky folk, and they will all be crushed to death. As you can see, there is no driver who might stop the trolley in time. Fortunately, there is a switch at hand, and if you throw the switch, you will divert the trolley onto a side track. Unfortunately, strapped to the rails on that track is another person. Throwing the switch would lead to that person's death. What would you do?

Lots of people think it's obvious. You should throw the switch and save the five. It's impossible to rescue all these luckless people, and it's better that five should survive, rather than only one.

Anyone who believes that the numbers always count will arrive at that verdict. So, provided you are already committed to a principle—it is always better to save the maximum possible number of lives—the answer is obvious. Yet the apparent point of the case, the rationale for the flourishing industry of Trolleyology, is to *test* that principle against intuitions. People who respond to the case simply by applying the principle to the situation aren't doing that. They are rather like my younger self, hopeless in laboratory experimentation, using the light from the window to estimate the focal length of the lens, and then (I confess) generating my "results" from the formula I was supposed to be testing.

What is supposed to happen is that belief in any principle is suspended. "Intuition" must operate uncontaminated by prior commitments. Unfortunately, though, our grasp of how "intuition" works is so rudimentary that you should feel quite uncertain about whether your "intuition" about the case is uncontaminated by your firm belief in the maximizing principle. In my embryonic career as a dry-labber, I had no difficulty in telling what I was doing: I knew I was fudging the numbers. Philosophers with firm allegiances to particular moral stances cannot be so clear about what is going on in generating their "intuitions." Reasonable skepticism should engender tentativeness about what the "intuitive" judgment is.

Indeed, "tentative" overstates the reactions of the uncorrupted. Perhaps my own experience in teaching undergraduates is unusual, but, in my efforts to present them with Trackside View and kindred cases, the main difficulty is eliciting any response at all. Almost everybody in the class shifts uneasily. When I look at particular people, eyes are lowered. If I press for an answer, I start to feel like the principal investigator in some notorious (and notoriously unethical) psychological experiment. There's no avoiding the conclusion. Unless they have prior commitments, "intuition" doesn't yield a firm answer. They would probably be even more reluctant to speak up if they knew how variable some, supposedly intuitive, moral judgments are across cultures and historical periods (as, for example, in differences between Chinese and American responses to the Trolley Problem).

Moreover, as I find out when I ask them to imagine being in the situation, there are good reasons for their hesitation. Life isn't like that—the predicament is "too weird." Anyone observing the people in danger would want to save them—*all* of them. So, once my students have expressed that thought, we can start to explore what they would do. They arrive to find the victims bound to the track. Can they set them free? No, I say, the bonds are too tight, there's no way to cut them, there's too little time. Can they signal someone to stop the trolley? No, they can see the empty cab. But how are they so sure that nobody is directing its course? They just are sure: it's certain that the trolley is running without any human control. Might there be people on the trolley, whose lives would be endangered if its course were diverted, and it went off track? No, you know that throwing the switch will work, and the trolley will continue on the other track. What about placing an obstacle between the five and the oncoming trolley? That can't be done, since there's nothing around you could use.

I keep imposing conditions, things the person at trackside can observe—or (more often) know by some other (unspecified and mysterious) means. Despite all my explanations, most of my class continues to balk. One student, more articulate than the others, typically closes the discussion in a way that prompts nods of assent: "OK. It's impossible to save everybody. You've built that into the case. But still, if you ask me how I would act, if I were beside the track, I'd search for some way of stopping the trolley. I wouldn't *know* that it's impossible, and I'd keep trying. At the last moment, in desperation, I might throw the switch, but I wouldn't see that as the *right* thing, only as the lesser of two bad options. I'd regard myself as having failed. I hadn't been sufficiently resourceful in finding a way out."

That response—and I've heard something like it several times—identifies a crucial difficulty with this kind of case. To make the case work, all kinds of constraints have to be imposed. Moreover, it's not enough for these conditions to *apply* in the envisaged situation—they also have to be matters about which the agent is completely *sure*. So a world is constructed, a "small world," one totally alien to the students' experience. Imaginative identification is blocked because they can't think themselves into a world with those properties, can't imagine being certain about all the things that force the alleged options for them. This world is just too small—it constricts them. They rightly resist the attempt to compel judgment when their capacities for judging find no purchase. So they lack the "intuitions" philosophers think they are supposed to have.

But it gets worse. Trackside View is only the beginning of wisdom in Trolleyology. My students are even more perplexed by a well-known follow-up case.

Runaway Trolley: Fat Man on Bridge
As in Trackside View, you see five people strapped to the rails and thus in danger from a runaway trolley. This time there is no side track, and no switch to throw. Instead, you observe the

situation from a bridge above the tracks. A fat man is sitting on the parapet of the bridge. If you were to push him off, he would fall into the path of the trolley, thus halting it before it would hit the five potential victims. Should you push the fat man?

Philosophers divide on this case. Some take it to fall under the scope of the "go by the numbers" principle and opt for pushing the fat man. Others take it to expose the limitations of the principle and refuse to sacrifice a presumably innocent observer. Undergraduates, at least those whom I have encountered, are even more adamant that they don't want to answer.

Completely understandably. For Fat Man on Bridge is even weirder than Trackside View. As in the latter case, various things have to be known for certain: the trolley is not controlled, there's no inanimate object to serve as an obstacle, no missile that might derail the trolley, no potentially vulnerable passengers. But more besides. You have to be sure:

That you are too light to serve as an obstacle (otherwise you could sacrifice yourself)

That the fat man would fall if you pushed him (otherwise your gesture would be useless)

That he would land in a place that would block the trolley (useless, again)

That he would not agree to leap, either alone or with you.

How you are supposed to become aware of these things is left unspecified. In fact, the difficulties of accounting for this alleged knowledge are spinoffs from a more fundamental bizarreness in the case. Why are you supposed to think of pushing the fat man as an option?

Perhaps the philosophers who claim to have clear intuitions about Fat Man on Bridge are different. But, like my students, when I walk around the world, spotting people, corpulent or not, on the parapets of bridges, I am not inclined to think of their potential as obstacles to impede runaway trolleys. Sometimes their seat strikes me as precarious, and I worry about their safety. Perhaps I should talk to them and advise them to come back down. Even if there were a runaway trolley bearing down on five people strapped to the track (and I rarely come across that kind of situation), the thought "You could always push the fat man" would not occur to me. I don't think this is an idiosyncrasy of mine.

So when I'm asked to consider what I'd do in Fat Man on Bridge, one of the supposed options isn't even on the cards. It's no good for the Trolleyologist to try to compel me to make up my mind by asking me to imagine that I see pushing the fat man as a possibility. I don't know what it would be like to see that. Even less do I know what it would be like to know (for certain) that there were only two possibilities—pushing the fat man, or allowing the five to die, the former certain to succeed. Like my students, like just about everyone, I can think myself into some scenarios and feel an inclination to identify with a particular course of action. But here the cognitive/affective gears don't mesh with the stipulations of the case. So, I believe, those without axes to grind are left nonplussed.

The standard philosophical name for the supposedly correct responses is "intuition." As I understand it, advocates of appealing

to judgments about hypothetical cases think of a process, initiated by imagining the favored scenario, something akin to everyday perception, and as issuing in justified assessments. There's no
well-established theory of how the process of intuition works or
of the circumstances under which it is reliable, but, for much of
human history, the same would have been true of vision, hearing,
taste, smell, and touch. The analogy between perception and intuition is imperfect, in that, even before people knew much about
the operation of the senses, they were reasonably clear about the
kinds of things being perceived and had some ability to tell when
a particular sense was being misled. If we are to take the analogy
seriously, and not simply dismiss the judgments elicited as idiosyncratic eruptions in human psychological lives, two features of
everyday perception are transferable to our thinking about intuition. First, children need to be taught to observe and to detect
particular kinds of objects, states of affairs, and events. The socialization they receive continues for some people, for artists and
fashion designers who need greater sensitivity to hues and tints,
for musicians whose ears are trained to identify pitches, pitch relationships, inner voices, and musical structures, for scientists who
must learn to see strata or cellular components or forms of animal
behavior. Second, sensed difficulty in sensing justifies withhold-
ing judgment or, at most, tentative judgment.

   These two points combine in the diagnosis I have offered of my
students' uneasiness when confronted with philosophical cases.
As those cases become too outré, the capacities, skills, and habits
stemming from their particular versions of our common adaptive psychology through processes of socialization and education,
break down, leaving them speechless. That isn't a mark of their

deficiency. It is, rather, a signal that, with respect to this particular scenario, intuition, whatever it's like, cannot function properly. The world envisaged is too remote from the world to which their capacities are adapted.

Aficionados might reply that philosophical training sharpens the intuitive ability. Perhaps. What is completely clear, however, is that philosophical training instills definite attitudes toward putative principles. An alternative to thinking that philosophers are the intuitional equivalents of the keen-eyed watchers of the skies who can detect heavenly motions lesser observers cannot distinguish is to suppose that "intuition" is molded by antecedent philosophical commitment, that what occurs in the philosophers' response isn't some higher power but the corruption of what is, among the folk, an unbiased faculty.

The method I have been reviewing has some obvious merit—when it is deployed judiciously. It is akin to techniques used in jurisprudence, where hypothetical cases are introduced to bridge the gap between some established precedent and a matter of current concern. Pinned down at both ends, the usage of a scenario is rightly debated by examining the strength of the similarities. Although philosophers cannot be as explicit about why they are making the judgment they do—they can't say, as a legal scholar might, that the newly introduced case is akin to one previously decided, only that their response to it is "intuitive"—they may try to justify their evaluations. In Drowning Child, for example, the familiarity of the situation allows people to imagine what it would be like to come across a child in danger, and to explain their responses as the smooth operation of the underlying capacities. (As I have noted, the moral debate centers on whether the scenario is connected closely enough—"pinned down"—to the program for giving Singer advocates.)

All goes reasonably well, then, when the scenarios remain close to our experiences. Sometimes, the agreement among very different people, together with the confidence resulting from the imaginative immersion, suggests that the judgment may be justified. That is also the case, I think, for another kind of storytelling, typically more complex than the tales philosophers construct, but manageable nonetheless. Great writers can construct fictional worlds, in which readers can submerge themselves, vividly imagining what it would be like to be a particular character in a particular predicament. Fiction, drama, and film can offer intricate presentations of decisions and conduct. As recent work in philosophical discussions of novels, plays, and movies has shown, these are sites at which difficult ethical issues can be explored.

Pathology starts where our inability to enter the scenario begins. Even before that, however, I would recommend a cautious rephrasing of the standard confident assertion. Instead of saying—as if one were reporting on an ordinary observation— "My intuition about Puzzling Case is . . ." philosophers would do better to avoid mentioning a process about which so little is understood. Why not say instead: "When I reflect on Puzzling Case, as a result of our common psychological adaptations and my particular history of social interactions, I find myself inclined to say . . . "? Longer and clumsier, to be sure, but humbler and more honest.

***

Let's briefly take stock. I've reviewed three pathologies: the fetish for complete clarity, the fetish for formalization, and the introduction of hypothetical cases, so far removed from reality as to defy imaginative identification. Before proceeding to my second trio, it's worth noting how these three are easily found in combination with one another.

Someone who seeks an analysis of a concept that will cover all possible cases, or the formulation of a principle that would hold in any possible situation, will be driven to test proposed analyses or available versions against any scenario an inventive mind can dream up. The enterprise of revising current proposals may start close enough to home to elicit confident responses about whether, under the circumstances considered, the test has been passed. Yet, given the goal of universality, the enterprise must leave the sphere within which imaginative identification can be achieved. The test cases introduced will come to include some ingenious fantasies with respect to which unbiased "intuition" yields no answer. At this point, aspiring authors committed to a particular analysis or principle often declare the test to have been passed, while others, with different affiliations, will see failure. Both sides are then inspired to generate more scenarios, ever more intricate and fanciful, in their endeavors to demonstrate the correctness of their response to the cases that provoke division. For any philosopher who has followed the career of a significant number of debates during the past several decades, the dynamic is surely familiar. Cases are multiplied. The analyses and principles become laden with qualifying clauses in attempts to accommodate the cornucopia of "intuitive evidence." Until, ultimately, the enterprise runs out of steam, and the case-mongers move on to fresh woods and pastures new.

Along the way, in a search for clarity as the logical structure of the proposal loses the transparency of the original suggestions, formalism may be wheeled in to refine what might otherwise become a vague or ambiguous formulation. Perhaps it will apply an already existing formal language. Or maybe something new will be required. Either way, the development is likely to be seen as positive. As progress.

A pathologist finds no great difficulty in summing up what has happened in this well-known story. Assuming that the first attempts to clarify the concept or to find an adequate principle addressed some genuine need (not, as we shall see, always a trivial assumption), the initial stages may have been helpful. They may have supplied all that was required to meet the original demands, fulfilling the purposes Peirce intended for his expositions. Yet the fetish of complete clarity drives the venture further. "Intuition" loses whatever purchase it once had. The result, then, is a recital in which performers play études of finger-tangling difficulty, whose musical value is, at best, nil.

These virtuoso performances should not drown out the real music.

***

What are the sources of philosophical knowledge? How can a philosopher justify a claim about what it is correct to do or what conditions are required for a state to be democratic? The approach just reviewed answers these questions. Philosophical method works through constructing hypothetical cases and reviewing them in intuition. Philosophers can pronounce from the armchair, in ways others cannot, because they are especially good at conjuring up a wide array of scenarios and subjecting them to the test of intuition. If, however, intuition is—at best—reliable only when the stories stay relatively close to the world of everyday experience, it is not so obvious why the community of philosophers is especially privileged with respect to the projects its members undertake.

Earlier generations of analytic philosophers might have answered the questions slightly differently. Instead of trying to prescribe a method, they could have specified the goal. Philosophy strives to uncover the structure of concepts, exposing semantic connections until everything is made completely clear. They might have continued by pointing to a number of exemplary efforts—by thinkers like Wittgenstein, Carnap, and J. L. Austin, whose efforts in this regard are rightly admired. Offering answers along these lines helps to distinguish philosophers' special talents from those of the folk, only to arouse a different query: why are philosophers better than lexicographers or linguists, when it comes to performing this task? Perhaps the (healthy) trend among some philosophers of language to engage more closely with work in linguistics represents an acknowledgment of the force of the challenge.

Let's pose the issue a bit more aggressively. Western philosophy has existed for over two millennia. For a very large part of that period, knowledge of many aspects of the world was the product of the efforts of people working in very different ways. Some of them we think of as philosophers. Others seem better classified as scientists or doctors or theologians or social theorists or lawyers or . . . . During the last few centuries, however, inquiry has made remarkable advances in any number of fields. Investigators come in many varieties. There are all kinds of specialists and subspecialists, equipped with all sorts of methods for addressing the questions with respect to which they are given responsibility in our division of investigative labor. If philosophy has no distinctive method of proceeding, why does it still survive? Why didn't it quietly fade away, when the domains it had once shared with others were handed over to different specialists? Perhaps, it should have withered in the eighteenth century, as soon as it became clear that knowledge of the world requires focused observation and experimentation. Philosophers are no more likely than other folk to engage in the kinds of contact with nature that can yield serious knowledge. Or maybe it could hang on a bit, simply because some fields—biology, psychology, economics, linguistics, political science—were latecomers to the Serious Inquiry Business? Now that they are here, however, why do universities continue to pay philosophers to do research? What do they contribute? *How* can they contribute anything of any worth?

What's the use of philosophy? In part, the question gains force from the suspicion that there aren't any special sources of philosophical knowledge. That suspicion is fueled by the apparent ineptness of philosophers to explain how they acquire any basis for their judgments. We seem to many people "just to be making it up."

In fact, the history I irreverently summarized reveals how, from the scientific revolution of the seventeenth century on, many of the greatest figures in the history of Western philosophy would have responded to the skeptical question. They would have insisted on the power of thought to generate certain kinds of knowledge (or, for some of them, to generate kinds of certain knowledge!). Descartes could sit down by the stove and arrive at enduring principles, beyond possible doubt, by meditating; Kant claims to have attained fundamental knowledge of important matters, knowledge that is "independent of all experience." Kant gave this species of knowledge the name under which it has since made its way in the philosophical world. It is a priori knowledge.

And has it ever made its way! Almost all philosophers think our knowledge of logic and of mathematics is a priori. (I am one of the exceptions to this view.) Many contemporary philosophers also believe that whatever they contribute to the store of knowledge is a priori. Unlike many of their predecessors who gave us coordinate geometry, or the calculus, or the economic advantages of free trade, or the nebular hypothesis, or solutions to problems in economics, or mathematical logic, or . . . , only a small percentage of philosophers today make contributions to other fields. They read, and sit, and think, and talk, and think again, and read again, and talk again, and think again . . . and write. Out of this process come their articles and books. Where, if at all, do the kinds of contacts with reality that undergird the knowledge of ordinary folk and of specialists in some area of science (broadly construed) help them come to new knowledge?

Possibly indirectly. Standard forms of experiential knowledge stand behind the claims of some of the authors they read, and, maybe, behind things they learn from some of their interlocutors. So the knowledge they contribute can't be entirely independent of experience, since they are indebted to the experiences of others (and—a banal point—to the processes through which their sources transmit information to them). Plenty of philosophers believe, nonetheless, that some of what they offer the world is a priori knowledge. For, in what they write, they sometimes hail a particular principle as "a priori." Typically, it is a thesis for which they supply no justification, but take as a premise in a line of argument. A *necessary* premise. Without it, they would not be able to reach their proffered conclusion.

What exactly do they mean when they characterize their theses as a priori? At least in the early parts of his *Critique of Pure Reason*, Kant is clear about what he has in mind. A priori knowledge is knowledge generated by processes of thought that could occur in the knower, whatever experiences she had had (provided only that they could suffice to teach her the concepts involved in the knowledge claim), that would sustain justification whatever her experiences, and that would invariably yield true belief (Kant 1787/1996; my interpretation is given in Kitcher 1980, another place in which I may have shown the influence of the fetish of formalism, and even of the fetish for complete clarity). Those are extremely strong conditions. Are they what the author of the journal article has in mind?

Almost certainly not. The author may well believe that the process through which he has arrived at his thesis is one he might have repeated, given any course of life experience (provided it was sufficiently rich). He *may* think the thesis is not merely true but could not have been false. He is, however, unlikely to suppose that any experience whatsoever would have enabled that process to yield justified belief. Our opinions are too easily undermined, our justifications unsettled by illusions, deceptions, apparently authoritative testimony, and the like. Let's say, then, that a claim is *weakly a priori* just in case it satisfies only Kant's first condition—the thought process generating it is always available, and if, given the experience the believer has, it is actually justified and actually true. I suspect that most of the authors who decorate the premises they introduce (without further support) as "a priori" have something like this in mind. If they do not, they owe the world some account of why they are using the term, since they appear to be rejecting all the conditions that their illustrious philosophical predecessors have placed upon it.

If, however, they declare their favored necessary premise to be weakly a priori, they have lapsed into a fourth pathology—I'll call it *sprinkling fairy dust*. For the effect of labeling Necessary Premise in this way (probably the intended effect) is to transform an unfamiliar and often ugly statement—a philosophical frog—into a gleaming philosophical prince. Wearing "a priori" Necessary Premise stands before the readers in full glory. No further questions need to be asked about its (his) credentials. Just look inward and reflect. The thought process should run its course in you, bringing the indisputable charm of Necessary Premise to your consciousness. If it does not . . . ? The defect is in you.

Claiming apriority is currently less popular than appealing to intuition about cases—but the two strategies are in the same line of work, and sometimes even fused together.[1] In both instances, they preempt objections to a thesis the author needs, if he is to elaborate his argument. I have already suggested a more accurate and more modest reformulation of "My intuition about this case is . . . ." The appeal to the a priori should also be recast. Instead of saying "Necessary Premise is a priori," it would be more straightforward to declare: "Necessary Premise is a judgment at which I have arrived after long reflection, and one that has survived my efforts to think of ways in which it might turn out false."

As authors surely understand, there are costs to saying that. My reformulation issues an invitation to ask questions, questions that could not be briefly answered. What reflections? What efforts? Without attaching an appendix—as mathematicians do when the proof is complicated, or as scientists do when they are asked to supply their data—the author couldn't explain how he's arrived at his firm conviction about Necessary Premise. Sprinkling fairy dust shortcuts all that. Hence the popularity of the practice.

Yet, sometimes, authors can do better. They can reveal what has actually convinced them of a particular principle or inclined them to characterize something in a specific way. A conversation I once had with a friend, one of the most creative and influential philosophers of science of our times, brought me to appreciate this point.

Until his death, Nancy Cartwright spent many years happily married to another eminent philosopher, Stuart Hampshire. One day, though, as Nancy and I were having lunch together, she said, with some irritation: "Stuart tells me I never give any arguments. Do I give arguments, Philip?" I thought for a little while, before replying. "Yes, Nancy, you do," I told her, "but they all have the same form—Here are some phenomena. Try looking at them this way." Again and again, throughout her writings, she offers her readers some facts about areas of scientific work or about social programs, sometimes unfamiliar, sometimes juxtaposing the familiar with the previously unrecognized, points to tensions among them or with standard judgments about them, and offers a perspective on them to resolve the tensions and to make sense of the whole. As I have since reflected on that conversation, I have begun to think she is not alone in coming to her innovative (and sometimes startling) views through this kind of argument—I'll dub it *modus Cartwright*, in her honor. It's all over the history of Western philosophy, at the moments when a thinker is introducing new principles and new concepts; also in many of the illuminating discussions authored by her (skeptical) husband. (And, as you might have observed, I've just made a very modest use of *modus Cartwright* in my own ruminations.)

So, perhaps, instead of the pathological sprinkling of fairy dust, the author would do better by claiming to be performing *modus Cartwright*. Even better, of course, if he were to give (as Nancy does) the goods. Reflecting on his route to Necessary Premise, he might recognize a cluster of phenomena that he found initially puzzling to which Necessary Premise brings order and coherence. So he might do better than make conversation-stopping appeals to the "a priori," or even to bald confessions of *modus Cartwright*. He could point to the considerations from which his affection for Necessary Premise emerged. Perhaps even with relative brevity. "Here are some phenomena," he might say, "Try looking at them this way."

***

When philosophers realize the extent to which their philosophical work depends on experience and on experiential knowledge, they are sometimes encouraged to make systematic use of ideas from some other area of inquiry. They see the potential for knowledge gained elsewhere to influence philosophical discussions. Another healthy impulse. But, again, one that can lead to pathology.

In this instance, the disease stems from underestimating the intricacies of the domain from which the philosopher proposes to borrow—or perhaps from overestimating the relative subtlety of philosophy. The venture into new intellectual territory is not so much a deliberate exploration, helped by wise local guides, as a snatch-and-grab raid. A prominent idea catches the philosophical eye. It is detached from all the connections that elaborate and qualify it. A cartoon emerges and becomes the basis of a long sequence of misguided philosophical writings. Furthermore, in the course of the ensuing discussions, the number of simplifications tends to grow, with the caricature becoming ever more distorted.

Darwin is especially vulnerable to this treatment. The central thought behind evolution by natural selection is simple—Huxley was right to exclaim "How stupid not to have thought of that!"— and so those who (knowingly, or not) agree with Dewey in recognizing Darwin's importance for philosophy (Dewey 1909/ 1998) sometimes clutch at the most elementary formulation. "A trait can only evolve," they declare, "if it yields some advantage to its bearer." Inspired by this declaration, they can try to put it to work. Some philosophical views, they claim, attribute properties to human beings that could not have brought any advantage to our ancestors. Those properties, therefore, could not have evolved. Any philosophical position committed to seeing them as part of our human nature is refuted.

During the past sixteen years, evolutionary debunking arguments have given rise to a thriving cottage industry. Journals are full of articles advancing or refuting attempts to discredit various philosophical theses. Ambitious undergraduates, keen on impressing graduate admissions committees, proliferate further versions of the genre—as I know, from having been asked to read so many of them for my own department. Very few, if any, of the numerous examples I have read show serious engagement with the details of Darwin's own views, let alone with the century-and-a-half's worth of refinement and elaboration that has occurred since the *Origin of Species*.

As so often in philosophy, the article initiating the trend was far subtler and more sophisticated in its treatment of evolution than those that have swum in its wake. Fifteen years ago, a gifted young philosopher published "A Darwinian Dilemma for Realist Theories of Value," an article in which she went considerably beyond cartoon Darwinism—"if it doesn't yield an advantage, it can't evolve!"—and took into account some of the respects in which the caricature might need modification (Street 2006). Her involvement with Darwinism did not, in my view, go far enough, and the argument was consequently flawed. But most of her successors have thrown all caution to the winds. With worse results.

Sharon Street's declared aim was to debunk moral realism, the view that correct moral judgments tell the truth about some independent moral realm. Her fire focused on any alleged capacity for detecting the features of this realm and adjusting action accordingly. Champions of moral realism tend to be coy. They are reluctant to say very much about the capacity (capacities?) in question, although so long as they attribute some moral knowledge and suppose conduct to be shaped by it, they must, it seems, believe it to exist. Some of their detractors are skeptical on non-evolutionary grounds, offering arguments to doom any possibility of acquaintance with the posited moral realm. Presumably Street and the debunkers who have followed her lead must take these arguments to be inadequate, since they turn to a Darwinian challenge to supplement or to replace them. Evolution is wheeled into the battle as heavy artillery: no account of the evolution of the hypothetical ability, the moral sense, could be provided; hence, it is not a capacity human beings could have come to have.

So long as you adopt a highly simplified view of Darwinian evolution, suspicions about a path from the amoral state to the hypothesized capacity are not hard to fathom. Wouldn't appreciation of moral truths lead people to make sacrifices, handicapping them in the reproductive competition on which the evolutionary trajectory depends? To amend the Anglican General Confession, morally praiseworthy tendencies will "incline them to leave undone what they ought to have done (to spread their genes), and make them do what they ought not to have done (to achieve reproductive success)—and there will be no evolutionary future for them."

Too simple. Giving the details of evolutionary explanations is notoriously difficult, especially when the trait whose presence is to be understood is complex. When, typically after years of sophisticated genetic and ecological studies, an investigator (or team of investigators) proposes an account, the investigator claims to have identified a number of things: the current form of the trait, the ancestral form in which the trait was absent, the ancestral environment, the changes (if any) in the environments experienced by the intermediate forms, a sequence of intermediates, and, in the most compelling cases, some features of underlying genotypes, with attention to the ways in which the pathway from genotype to phenotype might affect other features of the organism, besides the focal trait. Someone who thinks a trait could not have evolved under natural selection must claim that, given the ancestral form and the environment(s) in which the organisms have lived, there is no sequence of intermediate forms on whom possession of the trait (in its intermediate forms) would have conferred an advantage. Usually, the skeptic thinks the trait would have been *dis*advantageous in its intermediate versions.

That, it seems, is how evolutionary debunking ought to work. That's the way it's done by those who are best at it. The real masters of the craft aren't philosophers. Indeed, they're people many of the philosophical debunkers despise. (Not all though—some respected philosophers, moved by a narrow, literalist, dogmatic Christianity, love to aim debunking arguments against traits human beings clearly have, thus "refuting godless evolution.") The virtuosi in evolutionary debunking are known to the world as "Creationists" or as proponents of "Intelligent Design."

The style of argument I have reviewed is evident in the well-known Creationist gibe "What use is half an eye?" The Creationist knows the current phenotype: he can draw on textbooks to explain the anatomy and physiology of eyes. The Creationist claims to identify an ancestral form, a remote predecessor with no sensitivity to light at all. How, the Creationist asks, do you get, in gradual stages, from that to this? Surely, along the way, there must have been large numbers of useless contraptions, interfering with all sorts of previously well-functioning organs and systems. It is, at least at first sight, a formidable challenge—indeed, one sufficiently powerful to have bothered Darwin. Yet, since the nineteenth century, the mystery has been solved, as researchers have found organisms with various capacities for responding to light and have constructed chains of modified forms to link distant eyeless ancestors with the seeing animals of today. Once-triumphant Creationists have had to retreat and to rely on other, less catchy, cases. The bacterial flagellum is one of their favorites.

Some bacteria have tails (flagella) that they move to propel themselves through ambient media. Others don't. The aspiring Creationist debunkers can use the unflagellated as models for the ancestors of the flagellated. They can explore the environments in which related members of both types live. Hence they can specify a fair number of details about the story they challenge Darwin's defenders to tell—here's the starting point, here's the endpoint, here's the environment along the way, with its various pressures on putatively evolving organisms; now tell us how the bacteria got from there to here! When they can specify this much, they deserve some sort of appreciation. Let's call cases in which these constraints can be fully characterized *high-end Creationist debunking*.

What's wrong with the Creationist argument? It overlooks a number of features of evolutionary theory, not only as it is practiced today (informed by information about dynamic genomes, for example) but that have been commonplaces for half a century. The evolution of a population is traceable in terms of gene frequencies. Individuals with new genotypes are produced. Whether a genotype increases in the population will depend (forgetting about a few possibilities that would complicate the Creationist's reliance on the idea that disadvantages are inevitably driven out) on whether the *overall phenotype* resulting from the genotype in that environment yields an advantage in reproduction (a greater number of descendants). A new genotype *may* only modify a single trait of the organism—but that would be highly unusual. Typically, genetic modifications affect a *bundle* of characteristics, and the new genotype will succeed if that bundle confers an advantage. Of course, the bundle may contain traits that would be disadvantageous if they were the sole phenotypic property to change. *A* plus *B* plus *C* organisms leave more descendants than the unmodified form, but if an organism just had *A* it would be less reproductively successful. Given the phenomenon of linkage, however, you don't just get *A*. Because of genetic-developmental pathways, the choice is between the whole package (*A*, *B*, and *C*) and the prior type. *A* plus *B* plus *C* wins, and *A* comes along for the ride.

So the Creationist idea of bacteria evolving by adding tiny bits of a tail (useless until you have the whole thing) is an arbitrary choice from a space of unknown possibilities. The impossibility of the evolution of the flagellum could only be demonstrated if further work were done, specifically exploration of the genetics underlying flagellal development. Until that is fully worked out, the debunking argument—even though it's high-end—is worthless speculation.

Let's turn back to philosophy and compare philosophers' debunking arguments with high-end Creationism. What constraints on the alleged problem for evolution can the philosopher specify?

None. Philosophers' debunking arguments are *bargain-basement* Creationism.

That's a strong charge. But justified. Can the philosopher tell us the current form of the moral realist's alleged capacity (or should it be "capacities"?) for detecting moral reality and acting according to what those who have it come to recognize—the psychological phenotype evolution under natural selection allegedly can't deliver? No. Moral realists are very cagey (vague) about this—their reticence (to repeat) could be grounds for concern about their position. But complaints about vagueness (or impossibility) can be made without dragging in Darwin. Is it possible to describe the ancestral population in which the first changes that might have initiated the evolution of the capacity occurred? In principle, perhaps. Were the philosophers to study the contributions of primatologists and archeologists—debunkers usually don't—they could learn many things about the characteristics, physical and, to a lesser extent, social and behavioral, of our predecessors. But to make use of that information, they would have to specify some rough time period during which the evolution of the moral sense is supposed to have occurred. Of course, nobody is prepared to do that, and hence the ancestral type of *Homo*, just before the initial emergence of the capacity, is left completely unspecified. Can our Creationist debunkers tell us anything about the selective environment in which they take the evolution of the capacity to occur? They could garner some information about Paleolithic human environments from the writings of outstanding scholars (again—they don't), but to make use of the findings they would have to fix on a time period. For there have been significant changes in the physical environments human beings have inhabited during the last two hundred thousand years—and, more crucially, changes in the social environments (this is, after all, a period during which human language is often supposed to have evolved) that would sometimes have transformed human behavioral repertoires.

What's being denied then? The possibility of some utterly vague psychological capacity evolving in a population of organisms whose properties are left almost totally unspecified, in environments about which we are told virtually nothing. In effect, the evolutionary debunking argument is a variation on the cheapest Creationist gibe: What's the use of half a moral sense—or even a whole one? Bargain-basement Creationism, indeed.

Yet there are reasons to place the philosophical Creationists even lower, in some deeper subbasement. Their fellows who focus on the bacterial flagellum are not subject to a reasonable demand, one I haven't yet mentioned, that applies to the evolution of human beings and some other animals. People only talk about bacterial *culture* in a rather specialized sense. They don't think of capacities being "culturally transmitted" across the generations— baby bacteria receiving instruction from wise elders. With our own species, matters are rather different. Cultural transmission clearly goes on among primates, and it has been carefully studied in our closest evolutionary relatives. Thus there's every reason to think of the evolution of traits in *Homo* throughout the entire history of our species as governed not only by natural selection but by cultural selection as well. Since the mid-1980s, students of human evolution have known two important things about the operation of two forms of selection in tandem. First, a population evolving under both natural selection and cultural selection may follow a different trajectory—and fix different traits—from one evolving under natural selection alone. Second, if a population reaches an outcome different from the one it would have attained under natural selection, that outcome may remain stable; it is not fated to revert to the state that natural selection, acting alone, would have generated.

So "What's the use of half a moral sense?" is an even cheaper gibe than its Creationist counterpart.[2] When someone denies the value of half an eye or half a flagellum, he is at least absolved of the need to attend to cultural transmission and cultural selection. Philosophers focused on the moral sense not only fall into the gaping traps that beset Creationist debunking—most obviously, the failure to recognize the linkage among phenotypic traits. They also completely ignore a special, but hardly unobvious, feature of evolution in many organisms, most notably and most spectacularly in human beings. People who engage in *free-subbasement* Creationist debunking—a whole industry of recent philosophers—have no Culture.

To do worse than the cheapest Creationists is quite an achievement. Not one, I think, of which many philosophers would be proud. The pathology comes about, of course, because the purveyors of these dubious goods, debunkers and the anti-debunkers who reply to them alike, have only a nodding acquaintance with the field on whose ideas they intend to rely. The moral of the story should be plain: When you want to borrow ideas from some other intellectual domain, do your homework. Read up. Talk to the natives. Don't shrug off advice to probe more deeply. Be aware of the possibility that your philosophical applications might produce a cartoon version of the ideas you claim to value. And take steps toward avoiding that.

Not only in the case of Darwin, of course. The point applies when you borrow from psychology or anthropology or art history or physics or . . . . The Darwinian case is prominent, because so

many people think they can understand Darwinian evolution—
and even sum it up in a single sentence.

They might ponder the advice Francis Crick enunciated as
"Orgel's second law": remember that evolution is much cleverer
than we are.

***

I come to the sixth and last of my pathologies, another disease
born of a healthy impulse. The starting point this time is a proper
respect for what previous philosophers have achieved. It is right
to suppose human inquiry to be a roughly cumulative process.
Even in the moments when former firmly entrenched beliefs are
abandoned, we hope to build on the efforts of our predecessors,
to make up, eventually if not immediately, the losses incurred by
jettisoning some principle or theory that guided their successful
research.

Appropriate respect for tradition inclines contemporary philosophers to continue the ventures of the past, to return to questions that have been singled out for philosophical discussion, to
take up the debates in which previous generations have engaged.
Deference to the elders should not, however, be unthinking. From
time to time—at least once in a philosopher's career—she should
pause to take stock. Is this question, or this debate, one that
remains worth pursuing?

Sometimes people devoted to "freedom in philosophy" resist
the question. Nobody can predict, they say, which intellectual
pursuits will lead to future benefits. Better, then, to let individual scholars, disciplinary communities, even whole fields, go in

whatever directions they choose. No need to justify working on questions others dismiss as pointless. Sources of good things are often found in surprising places.

If investigative talent were widely cultivated across our species, allowing for all the perplexities and difficulties afflicting human beings to receive thorough attention, this plea for liberty might be persuasive. As matters stand, however, it is a rationalization for academic irresponsibility, for airy refusal of that "social division of labor" on which Dewey insisted. Surely, it "proves" too much. Should societies grant blanket permission to people who, in at least some instances, are privileged in the level of support they enjoy, to pursue any venture that arouses their intellectual curiosity, without any responsibility to account for the benefits they take it to deliver? In everyday life, an "anything goes" approach to planning is typically a luxury. Dickens saw the point clearly in his portraits of two feckless characters: Harold Skimpole (of *Bleak House*) and the better-known (and larger-hearted) Mr. Micawber (*David Copperfield*). Both of them glory in going where fancy takes them and they rely on others to support them when their confidently pursued (but optimistically designed) projects come crashing down—or simply fizzle. Unlike Skimpole, Micawber has real charm. So, too, may some philosophical rhapsodies about the unworried pursuit of projects whose probability of adding to the broader human good is infinitesimal. Yet those rhapsodies, and the "no questions asked" attitude they encourage, also exhibit the dark side of Micawberism.

Because it is Micawberish (or Skimpolean?), the libertarian defense fails to rebut the challenge to contemporary Anglophone philosophy to reflect far more often, and in greater depth, on the value of the questions about which "core philosophers" obsess. Socialized into a profession, too many young philosophers rarely scrutinize the worth of the enterprises to which they will devote years of their lives. Perhaps this is the most obvious pathology of all, apparent to those outsiders who learn about what their friends in the philosophy department are doing and wonder why anybody would want to find out about *that*. Besides the appeal to freedom, there's another standard reply. Philosophy has its own questions. Some of them are timeless. If the "core issues" do not move nonphilosophers, that is a sign of their ignorance and philistinism. The cognoscenti sniff, and continue with their exploration of the higher matters, unappreciated by the base vulgar.

Ever since Plato (or maybe Socrates), philosophy has posed plenty of "What is . . . ?" questions. The point of seeking answers to such questions is frequently to advance an investigation. For the first half of the twentieth century, geneticists offered several accounts of what genes are, and they were able to develop genetics further as a result. Yet mysteries remained. How could these mysterious entities lose one of their functions (generating abnormal phenotypes) while retaining another (copying themselves so they could be transmitted to progeny)? After Oswald Avery and his colleagues had identified DNA as the genetic material, James Watson and Francis Crick were inspired to investigate the structure of DNA, and molecular biology has since transformed our understanding of living organisms. Toward the end of their epoch-making article, Watson and Crick inserted a laconic sentence pointing toward a resolution of the mystery I have noted: "It has not escaped our notice that the specific pairing we have postulated suggests a possible copying mechanism for the genetic material."

Answers to "What is . . . ?" questions are seldom as fruitful as the one Avery and his coworkers provided. But, I suggest, we can assess the significance of questions by the size of the obstacles we expect them to remove. In this light, let's examine the relative significance of two questions that go back a long way in the history of Western philosophy.

"What is justice?" retains its importance. We know there is much we don't know about justice. That's clear from a host of disagreements about what counts as just treatment in a variety of contexts—when individuals interact with other individuals, when individuals interact with social institutions, when the state sets up (or amends) a framework for governing its citizens. Careful and wide-ranging accounts of justice are always welcome. By contrast, it's hard to see what any new answer to "What is knowledge?" would do for us. Would it aid people to make more accurate assessments of what they know and what they don't know? Not unless it were conceived as explaining what counts as evidence for beliefs in various domains—and giving those kinds of explanations would appear to be the province of the practitioners in those domains, and of those who study the methods deployed there (reflective practitioners and philosophers concerned with that specific sort of inquiry). Would it help investigators gain new knowledge or enable them to proceed at a faster rate? Probably not. Innovative methodological advice is always welcome, but, again, that's the province of people who understand specific kinds of inquiries. Answers about knowledge in general have nothing to say to them. Unlike the parallel question about justice, "What is knowledge?" is idle.

Analytic epistemologists may see this as yet more vulgar philistinism. Crude nonphilosophical folk don't appreciate the value of understanding "for its own sake." Dewey anticipated that line of defense and issued a diagnosis. He claimed that intellectual work should conform to a social division of labor, in which the inquiries conducted should serve others outside the tiny coterie of those who undertake them. When the connections to broader interests are severed, what remains is "a kind of intellectual busy-work carried on by socially absentminded men." There are all sorts of things people might want to know "for their own sake," and the choices of which ones to pursue ought to respond to interests that are widely shared. Otherwise, what results is a narcissistic elitism—or, as Hilary Putnam once put it to me (more bluntly), a form of mental masturbation.

The same pathology infects not only efforts to "clarify important concepts" but philosophical controversies about doctrines as well. For at least two decades, a significant percentage of discussions in ethics have centered on the issue of moral realism. Debates about the merits of evolutionary debunking arguments are only one part of a far larger cluster of exchanges. Moral realists contend that moral statements are true or false in virtue of some aspect of reality. On their account, moralists are attempting to fathom this facet of reality and to characterize it accurately, just as various other groups of investigators attempt to expose features of the natural or the social world.

Moral philosophy has its roots in a desire to improve human decision-making, human conduct, and the institutions that shape our lives. Contemporary normative ethics renews the reformist impulse, and it is one of the philosophical ventures whose contributions to society-wide discussions are broadly appreciated. Metaethics, the enterprise of investigating what ethical statements mean and what, if anything, makes them true or false, arises as a spin-off from this readily comprehensible project of reformation. To become clearer about the meanings of moral judgments might, by analogy with Avery's biological breakthrough, streamline normative discussions. Insight into the status of morality looks to be a promising source of better methods for generating and justifying theses about what people and institutions ought to do and be. As a side benefit, it would provide a rejoinder to those irritating skeptics (serious or not) who denounce moral principles as expressing arbitrary human demands, typically made in the interests of retaining power.

After more than a century of meta-ethical explorations, prominent among them debates about moral realism, what exactly has been learned? Suppose that, tomorrow, the philosophical community arrived at an unusual consensus: Moral realism is correct. What would be the payoff? Extraordinarily little. For the versions of moral realism proposed are either tailored to fit existing normative theories (utilitarianism, for example) that are, to put it mildly, controversial, or else so nebulous as to provide zero guidance in normative discussions. We are hardly advanced by learning that moral reality is something the author knows not what, accessed he knows not how, or even by the slightly more definite thought of morality as characterizing "what we have, overall, most reason to do." Linking morality to a realm of reasons is useless without some more definite account of what reasons are, one that might enable us to arrive at firmer judgments about where "the balance of reasons" lies, and thus devise methods for settling moral disputes more reliably and more systematically than we currently can. Nor is the response to the skeptics worth much. We can easily envisage their reply. "Do you really expect anyone to be confident about the existence of a supposed moral reality, concerning which your accounts are so thin? Odd, isn't it, that you insist it exists, while confessing your profound ignorance about its character or about how we find out about it?"

As my late colleague and friend, Isaac Levi, used to maintain—and he finally convinced me—arguments about realisms are worthless unless they have some methodological implications. In this instance, the meta-ethical turn began in hopes of illuminating normative disputes through ventures in semantics and ontology. It has come out *not quite* empty. But as near as makes no difference.

Yet my diagnosis, in this instance, has a positive message, too. For, once the tale I have briefly rehearsed is clearly appreciated, there's an obvious way to reform meta-ethics: give up the intricate exchanges about meaning and truth; focus instead on improving whatever methods we have for making moral progress.

"But how can you do that if you don't know what you're talking about?" Easy. Mathematicians and natural scientists do it all the time (recall Russell's famous remark about mathematics as "the subject in which we never know what we are talking about, nor whether what we are saying is true"). They develop new concepts, as well as new methods, by reflecting on the achievements of the past, and on the procedures that did and didn't work. Philosophers interested in moral methodology can do the same. Consider historical paradigms of what you take to be moral progress, look for features that advanced the progressive changes, as well as for those that retarded them. Formulate tentative methodological guidelines. Test them against further instances. Refine the methodological advice. Repeat.

I have tried, elsewhere, to present a first attempt at how this might work. Perhaps the turn to methodology might point meta-ethics toward a new question, one capable of delivering something to satisfy the reformist impulse that prompted meta-ethics in the first place (Kitcher 2021a).

***

Although pathology reports sometimes bring relief, they frequently prove upsetting. I fear that my review of philosophical pathologies will fall into the latter category, provoking distress and even outrage. The mirror I have held up to professional Anglophone philosophy has been constructed to make vivid the deformities I recognize in that academic practice, misshapen features that amuse or annoy or appall scholars in other fields. It is, of course, possible that the distortions are produced by the mirror itself—effects of the kinds produced by the reflective surfaces found in fairgrounds. Whether or not that is so, I hope my fellow philosophers will reflect on how their work may look from different angles and begin a serious interrogation of whether those perspectives expose a genuine defect.

Receiving bad news sometimes moves people to engage in denial. The report is seen as exaggerating the defects, failing to recognize positive features of the status quo, suffering from a dyspeptic lack of sympathy that generates blind spots and incomprehension. So complaints are waved away, and business goes on as usual. Philosophers all-too-easily take themselves to have grounds for dismissal. After all, their training in analysis and argument has equipped them with powerful weapons for use in disputes (or conversations) with colleagues from other disciplines, instilling a sense of intellectual superiority. "Smart" is a principal adjective when they rate one another, when they evaluate fellow academics, and even when they reflect on their personal acquaintances. Hence arises a professional culture with a tendency to assume that philosophers are usually (almost always?) "the smartest people in the room." Most of us have been guilty of succumbing to the lure of that attitude. Humility and the recognition of a diversity of cognitive and affective virtues would be wiser. So, too, would be an openness to self-examination and to questioning whether charges of pathology are altogether unfounded. My report is offered not as the last word on the state of contemporary analytic philosophy, but as an invitation to take its current health far more seriously than most philosophers are inclined to do. To induce a group of dedicated and highly talented people to reflect on what they are doing with their lives.

Moreover, as the discussion of moral realism is intended to bring out, identifying pathologies is not always negative. Beyond the obvious advice about the road to health—remove the offending feature—it is sometimes possible to point in a positive direction. So my remarks on idle "enduring questions" end with a suggestion about more profitable forms of inquiry.

In any event, we have lingered too long among the sick. It is time to respond directly to my title question and to paint a picture of philosophical health. What *is* the use of philosophy?

4 | THE WHOLE FUNCTION OF PHILOSOPHY

> The whole function of philosophy ought to be to find out what definite difference it will make to you and me, at definite instants of our life, if this world-formula or that world-formula be the true one.
>
> —*William James (James 1907/1975, 30)*

The sentence that supplies the title for this chapter is the third and last of a short paragraph in William James's seminal *Pragmatism*. It is far less often quoted than its predecessor, which presents a theme many scholars have seen as central to the pragmatist movement: the idea of there *being* no difference that doesn't *make* a difference to "somebody, somehow, somewhere and somewhen." The three sentences of that paragraph were important to James. They all occur in a much longer passage in the lecture in which he initially announced "the pragmatic method," a lecture delivered almost a decade earlier (at what was then known as "the University of California") and first published six years after it was given (James 1904/1978).

Even more explicitly in that earlier lecture, James's goal was to point out how philosophical disputes can easily collapse into

What's the Use of Philosophy? Philip Kitcher, Oxford University Press. © Oxford University Press 2023. DOI: 10.1093/oso/9780197657249.003.0004

insignificance, how philosophers can go on talking indefinitely about topics that have not the slightest bearing on what matters to other people. Many of their professional discussions today are not only irrelevant to the lives of the kinds of people among whom I grew up but also to the lives of my nonphilosophical friends and of my colleagues in other departments at the universities in which I have taught. Contrary to some interpreters of the pragmatists, James's dominant concern wasn't to present some improved theory of meaning—he didn't have advance access to Michael Dummett's thesis that the theory of meaning lies at the heart of contemporary philosophy. His target was much more straightforward. In his view, a lot of the philosophy he knew was insignificant—unimportant, not worth the time of talented and industrious people. Pragmatism, as he conceived it, would reform that.

The three sentences follow a natural sequence. First, diagnosis: a large amount of philosophical writing and talking "collapses into insignificance." Second, justification: it makes no difference to human lives (except, of course, to the lives of the tiny coterie who do the talking and the writing). Third, positive suggestion: James points to what, in his view, philosophy ought to do.

Contemporary philosophers, at least those who spend any time on James, often try to domesticate him, turning the second sentence into the sketch of a theory of meaning (a theory most of the would-be domesticators view as a disastrously bad one). They shy away from the explicit indictment of the first sentence and avert their eyes (to spare James's blushes?) from the language of the third. "World-formulas" indeed!

James was far from the first to feel a need to scrutinize the worth of philosophical projects. At the end of the *Enquiry Concerning Human Understanding*, David Hume proposes a program of philosophy book burning. Writings dealing with "relations of ideas"—treatises in logic and mathematics—should be preserved. So, too, for works offering factual information about the natural or social world. All the rest should be committed "to the flames" because they "can contain nothing but sophistry and illusion." Hume's peroration would be echoed, a decade or so after James's death, in the logical positivists' campaign for the elimination of metaphysics. The difference between James's diagnosis and that shared by Hume and the positivists turns on alternative readings of an ambiguous word: "significant." For Hume and company (including, allegedly, the properly domesticated James) much of philosophy is insignificant in the sense of being literally meaningless. For the real James, and even more explicitly for John Dewey, philosophy, as often practiced, lacks significance because it is unimportant, and the unimportance shows up in the lack of any impact on people's lives.

As previous chapters have noted, Dewey's writings contain many elaborations of James's diagnosis. *Democracy and Education* charges that philosophy may not only suffer from being "merely verbal" but also become "a sentimental indulgence for a few" (Dewey 1916/1975, 338). Five years later *Reconstruction in Philosophy* amplifies the charge. Dewey reflects on academic life, noting how it represents a "social division of labor." The division, he thinks, only proves healthy when those who pursue "theory and knowledge" are "in unobstructed cooperation with other social occupations, sensitive to others' problems and transmitting results to them for wider application in action." Without such connection, inquiry "easily degenerates into sterile specialization, a kind of intellectual busy work carried on by socially absent-minded men." When these people are challenged on the point, their "occupation is 'rationalized' under the lofty name of devotion to truth for its own sake" (Dewey 1920/1982, 164).

I hope the preceding chapters serve as an elaboration of James's and Dewey's negative work, the work of diagnosis, in the context of contemporary philosophy in the English-speaking world. The aim of this one is to develop further the positive account of philosophy they offer as a replacement.

***

Before constructing my preferred version of the James-Dewey picture, it is worth taking a look at the most perceptive response offered by those who reject pragmatist diagnoses of philosophy's ills. For any rival to orthodox conceptions will be improved by capturing whatever insights are presented by opponents of sweeping reforms.

A decade or so ago, a precursor of Chapter 1 (Kitcher 2011) plainly struck a chord with some readers. Equally, it appeared to many others as profoundly misguided, failing to appreciate the subtler values of Anglophone philosophy as it is practiced, as if I were some philistine outsider who had wandered in to an exquisite art collection and, after gawking uncomprehendingly, bluntly denounced what I had seen. I compared professionally high-status enterprises unfavorably with others, pursuits often regarded as "peripheral"—perhaps "worthy enough," but not "core philosophy." The pathologies identified in that original article, and at greater length in the preceding chapters, contrasted with my enthusiastic embrace of discussions about race and gender, of attempts to develop a methodology for causal analyses of statistical data, of studies of rationality and its limits, and of the genre of philosophical work about literature and music inspired by Stanley Cavell.

No more needs to be said about the negative case. The previous chapters may be too much already! Yet, since thoughtful people have found my "inside-out" vision wrongheaded, and even offensive (I apologize for my past—and present—lack of tact), it's worth offering a brief update to explain my enthusiasm for allegedly "peripheral" enterprises and my delight in seeing more of them flourish.

Today, at a time when political discussions are clouded by talk of "alternative facts," one might have thought that philosophical clarification of such claims could help. Most of the work in "core analytic epistemology" is unhelpful for these purposes. Nevertheless, a number of philosophers have provided illumination in work that is either socially informed (investigations of propaganda, for example; Stanley 2015) or develops formal models in social epistemology (studies of the ways in which information and misinformation flow through different kinds of social networks; O'Connor and Weatherall 2019).

Moreover, the value of philosophical studies of race is even clearer today than it was a decade ago. The sophistication of the contributions that have been made in this area, by philosophers developing critical race theory, by eliminativists and social constructivists, and by those exploring the biological and demographic phenomena underlying attempts to draw divisions within the human population, has increased enormously. Thanks to a whole alphabet of philosophers, from Anthony Appiah at the beginning to Naomi Zack at the end—with people like Robert Gooding-Williams, Sally Haslanger, Charles Mills, and Tommie Shelby in between—not only has the understanding of race and racism been decisively advanced, but there's good reason to think the progress has had an impact on public discussions.

In this chapter, I come to praise philosophy, not to bury it. During the years since I wrote "Philosophy Inside Out," a higher proportion of American philosophers have written articles and books illuminating issues for a broader public. Besides the examples I have already mentioned, other obvious ones include many contributions, offered by philosophers of all ages and with many different perspectives, to the *New York Times*' "Stone" column, Laurie Paul's studies of transformative experience (Paul 2014), Susan Neiman's reflections on coming to terms with a nation's horrific past (Neiman 2019), and the important work on epistemic injustice that has pursued issues pioneered earlier by Miranda Fricker (Fricker 2007). The health of the social division of labor is better than it was a decade ago.

So I am less pessimistic than I used to be. In the interests of revealing myself to be a reforming character—a philosophical philistine on the road to finer appreciation—I want to take up a line of thought suggested by people who believe I debase philosophy in the search for extra-philosophical relevance. These people would, I believe, endorse my admiration for the kind of work toward which I have gestured. Perhaps they now have a higher appreciation of the value of "applied philosophy" than they once did. But, they insist, that kind of work is not everything. It leaves out important kinds of studies philosophers pursue. A world in which philosophy is reduced to the ventures that make immediate social impact would have lost something important.

I agree wholeheartedly. On this point, my critics are entirely correct. My earlier account was incomplete. But I don't think the "enduringly significant core" of philosophy is what they think it is. James saw more, and saw more clearly, than those who protest my philistinism.

***

The real importance of that much-read paragraph lies in the final sentence—specifically in the question it attempts to answer. What is "the whole function of philosophy"?

James's own answer probably strikes you as somewhat odd—at least, I hope it does. References to "world-formulas" conjure up disconcerting images, inviting us to think of earnest seekers climbing mountains to receive from the solitary guru seated at the top the one-sentence answer to the "ultimate question." James's position can be clarified by following a thread leading from his early writings to the opening lecture of *Pragmatism*. "The Sentiment of Rationality" already foreshadows his later view of the whole function of philosophy:

> What is the task which philosophers set themselves to perform; and why do they philosophize at all? Almost everyone will immediately reply: They desire to attain a conception of the frame of things which shall on the whole be more rational

than that somewhat chaotic view which everyone by nature carries about with him under his hat. (James 1879/1979, 57)

In the first lecture of *Pragmatism*, the thought is further developed by taking these individual conceptions "of the frame of things" to have links to two major types of philosophical temperaments— the tough- and tender-minded. So, in the passage on which I am focusing, "world-formula" appears to refer to articulations and elaborations of these temperaments, philosophical systems whose deliverances may help people improve and refine the muddled— "somewhat chaotic"—approaches to life they "carry about under their hats."

The Dedication to *Pragmatism* hails John Stuart Mill as "our leader were he alive today," and I detect Mill's influence on James's proposals. *On Liberty* celebrates individual projects or plans of life, as later philosophers like Bernard Williams and John Rawls would call them (Williams 1981; Rawls 1999). Our free choice and pursuit of our projects constitutes, Mill claims, "the only freedom worthy of the name" (Mill 1859/2008, 17). His insistence on multiplying "experiments of living" points to a suggestion about how autonomous and intelligent choices are made: through recognition of the diverse ways in which people think of the world they inhabit and of their places in it, and subsequent attempts to derive an identity suited to the nascent individual. James adds to this picture the sensible thought that the resultant conceptions are likely to be something of a mess. Philosophy tries to proceed more systematically. It attempts to develop overarching accounts of "how things, in the broadest sense of the term, hang together, in the broadest sense of the term" (to use Wilfrid Sellars's influential and much-cited characterization of "the aim of philosophy" [Sellars 1963, 1]). James steps back from that creative project to recognize more modest goals. In the spirit of pragmatism, he supposes that the grand ventures are worthwhile only if they are connected with human lives, if they make a difference to "somebody, somehow, somewhere and somewhen." If "chaotic" conceptions are to be improved, people need to see how the large synthetic schemes (assumed to be articulations of two major species of temperaments) bear on their decisions and actions.

I shall want to clarify and refine this picture, but, even in the outline I've given, it will help me to respond to the thoughtful line of criticism to which I've referred. Readers of my early version of Chapter 1 have noted how that article conceives of philosophical relevance in a very direct, and thus restricted, way. Other areas of human inquiry have a problem. They send for the philosopher, in much the way homeowners might send for a plumber, to fix things. (Or, quite often, the philosophical plumber turns up, uninvited.) My critics rightly point to the many occasions on which successful research in coping with difficulties comes about in a more roundabout fashion. My own favorite instance derives from the history of genetics. After the rediscovery of Mendel's ideas in 1900, some geneticists were eager to apply the new approach to fathom hereditary human diseases. Over a century later, many important advances have been made in this area. They did not emerge, however, from any direct assault on the problem, but from a long and circuitous route through basic science—through developing genetic tools applicable first to fruit flies, to yeast, bacteria, and bacteriophage, through the identification of DNA as the hereditary material in most organisms, through understanding the molecular structure of DNA, cracking the genetic code, discovering precise techniques of gene mapping and sequencing, and, most recently, inventing molecular scissors-and-paste for modifying genomes. Surely we should want to applaud T. H. Morgan and his students for the groundbreaking work they did in the "fly room" at Columbia—and, by the same token, it is suggested, we should not dismiss the efforts of philosophers who tackle "core questions," often in ways quite remote from the urgent demands of the age.

There is, I think, genuine insight in this objection. Some philosophical projects without any direct bearing on extra-philosophical questions can be justified. Obvious examples occur in aesthetics and in the philosophy of science, where more abstract questions about artworks and aesthetic experience, or about confirmation and causation, can be expected to feed back into work that will illuminate particular types of works of art or prove valuable in clarifying urgent scientific controversies. As I'll suggest below, the most insightful contributions to the history of philosophy can be given a parallel defense. Nevertheless, to concede these points is not to issue a blank check. Those inclined to dispense the funds might ask how long it is proper to wait for the expected returns.

When you turn to the kinds of philosophical cottage industries I have targeted—large swaths of analytic epistemology, analytic metaphysics, and analytic meta-ethics—any such evident connection vanishes. The extra-philosophical world has been waiting a long time for the goods to be delivered. Is it reasonable to maintain that discussions of ever more far-fetched hypothetical scenarios will eventually contribute enhanced abilities to advance human knowledge, or the type of understanding metaphysics is supposed (wrongly, I think) to provide, or to guide individuals or societies to better decisions and improved conduct? That strikes some people, including me, as very hard to sustain. I vividly remember an occasion, at an interdisciplinary conference on knowledge across a variety of areas of inquiry, when, after the sole session devoted to analytic epistemology, the nonphilosophical researchers, drawn from many fields, erupted in outrage at the discussion they had just heard. One eminent psychologist brutally advised one of the participants to find "an honest line of work." That was cruel, but it was not hard for people who grew up, as I did, at a far remove from academia, to understand the impulse from which it flowed. We should not spend our time playing irrelevant games for "socially absent-minded" people. Sometimes our cottage industries may need an industrial revolution. Do professional philosophers fail to hear the stirrings of discontent because so many of them are academically and socially isolated? Or is it from a conviction that philosophers are *obviously* "the smartest people in the room"?

***

My diagnoses are, of course, fallible. Perhaps there is more kinship between "core philosophy" and the practices of the pioneering geneticists than I have allowed. Possibly some champion of the ventures I criticize will show how they help discharge the "whole function of philosophy." Perhaps the champion will demonstrate their bearing on some particular field of inquiry. Or, more likely, what will be shown is their pertinence to the function James identifies. From these explorations will come something—some thesis, some concept, some method—useful to people as they try to make sense of themselves and their world, a resource enabling them to remedy some part of the chaos bubbling away under their hats. I am doubtful. Yet, let me retreat further, reformulating my concern.

What prompted me to write "Philosophy Inside Out" was a sense that, all too often, questions about the worth of a professionally approved enterprise do not even arise. As I have just conceded, maybe a sterling defense could be given. What is problematic—*philosophically* problematic—is that it *isn't* given, and it isn't given *because the question never even surfaces*. Philosophers are socialized into the ways of a profession, taking it for granted that such-and-such is a "major philosophical question," even "one for the ages," and people spend years seeking answers without serious reflection on the sources of its significance. That strikes me, as it once struck Dewey, as a profoundly unphilosophical attitude. My aim is not to denounce, as if I were qualified to issue a final verdict on the value of particular practices. It is to raise skeptical questions, and thereby prod confident people to take an outside look at the research they do, to consider how it might (or might not) contribute something of value to the wider world, and thereby assess its worth *for themselves*. To ask themselves if they are in "an honest line of work." Self-examination of this kind is all too rare.

Professional philosophy can do better. Articulating James's view of "the whole function of philosophy" will help us consider how.

***

Some themes from Dewey suggest a more comprehensive answer to James's question. Dewey didn't suppose philosophers to have some special source of knowledge, or even some special method. Other academic disciplines, from anthropology and art history at the beginning of the alphabet to zoology at the end, engage in *first-order inquiry*. They aim at finding true answers to significant questions—or, as Catherine Elgin has eloquently argued, to answers that are "true enough" (Elgin 2017). Part of their task, though, is to identify *which* questions are significant, and in discharging this task (as I've tried to show during the past twenty years) they need to acknowledge the predicaments and aspirations of all members of our species (and of other sentient beings).

You can't hope to arrive at the *whole* truth about nature. There are at least continuum many true statements about the area in which you are sitting during the time through which you read this page—and only a tiny number of those, if any, are worth knowing. (How much would you really want to find out about the values of physical, chemical, and biological magnitudes at each of the space-time points in this interval of your life, about the relations among them, the relations among average values in all the many regions one could demarcate, and so on?) One of philosophy's tasks, I believe, is to assist the various areas of inquiry in their work of identifying significance, and to do so through helping people discover what most matters to them—sorting out the chaos under all those hats. As Dewey memorably puts it, "[Philosophy] is a liaison officer between the conclusions of science and the modes of social and personal action through which attainable possibilities are projected and striven for" (Dewey 1929/1984, 298).

Although I think that formulation needs adjustment, the figure is apt. For it draws our attention to the way in which philosophy finds its place *among* disciplines and *among* all the mess of the varied lives people live. Dewey sometimes puts the point, vaguely but suggestively, by saying that investigators, within institutionalized forms of inquiry and in the everyday activities of human life, find out lots of diverse facts—philosophers, reflecting on these, are to provide some account of the *"meanings"* of those facts (Dewey 1925/1981, 307). I read Dewey's loaded word—"meanings"—through the lenses offered by James and by Sellars. Philosophy strives for some kind of synthetic vision. Perhaps that is done, as James proposes, by taking some existing framework, offered by a philosophical system, and showing how it bears on lives in the here and now. Or perhaps it is pursued through Sellars's apparently more ambitious enterprise, finding a new synthesis of what is known and experienced, one that fits the times. Dewey would, I think, applaud both of the recommended ventures—*if* he felt either to be feasible. More thoroughgoing in his pragmatism than either James or Sellars, he sees their characterizations as ideals— and he views ideals not as terminal states toward which we ought resolutely to march, but as diagnostic tools, for appraising our current situation, uncovering problems, and initiating efforts to overcome our difficulties.

So Dewey, as I read him, diverges from James at the very end of the crucial sentence. He isn't allergic to talk of a "world-formula," but he worries about the idea of our ever finding one and is skeptical of regarding any such formula as "true." Humanity needs the synthetic thinking which both James and Sellars commend as philosophy's task. *But it is vastly overambitious to conceive*

this as directed at all-encompassing theories, capable of being true.
Think instead, he advises, about particular domains of human
life, about the sciences, the arts, political institutions, economic
frameworks, religious practices, education, and so forth. Reflect
on what is known in the areas on which you focus, and how it
relates to other parts of human life. So, for example, you might
want to assess the goals of education in light of the existing political or economic constraints, asking whether reforms are needed,
not to implement the currently identified political or economic
desiderata, but rather to change the entire framework (Dewey
1916/1975; Kitcher 2021b). What the philosopher supplies is a
more general view: posing questions, offering concepts, suggesting useful analogies, putting forward ideals. If you read Dewey in
this way, there will be no mystery as to why he writes the kinds of
books he does, unphilosophical as they seem to many. His books
are notably short on references to "the latest journal literature"—
not, of course, a body of work that has figured particularly often
in the genesis of the greatest works of philosophy that have ever
been written. Moreover, he typically introduces figures from the
history of philosophy only for the purposes of revealing how some
idea—usually one with advantages and defects—has been introduced and has shaped the ways in which people run their lives.
Like Nietzsche and Foucault, Dewey sometimes indulges in genealogy, doing so for the purposes of recognizing how we might liberate ourselves from constraints our predecessors have imposed on
us, in their own prior attempts to do the synthetic work he views
as philosophy's principal contribution.

So the worrying Jamesian idea of a "world-formula" is scaled
back a little. In many of his works, Dewey develops his version

of the "whole function of philosophy" by linking it specifically to the advance of inquiry. Philosophy is in the business not simply of responding directly to the problems and controversies of the age—the kind of work emphasized when philosophy is turned inside out—but also in helping with the general project of inquiry by working among various disciplines, developing conceptual tools to remove potential obstacles. For all their apparent failures, Hempel and his logical empiricist successors have sometimes helped the natural sciences in this way. So, too, writers about art and music have offered new ways of thinking about genres of art and their histories (Danto 1964, 1981, 1997; Goehr 2007). Even more influential have been the reshapings offered by John Rawls and Thomas Kuhn.

Yet, in this Deweyan articulation of the link between philosophy and human lives, something James perceived starts to disappear. Philosophers as liaison officers, or as handmaidens to other forms of knowledge seeking, are not entirely detached from the lives of ordinary folk. For the impacts they have on the various species of inquiry may resonate further, reaching a wider human population who are affected directly by the advances of the various investigations philosophy nurtures. When he specifies his conception as one of refining methods of inquiry, Dewey preserves an *indirect* connection to everyday life. James wanted more than that. I do, too.

***

In scaling back the bothersome idea of a world-formula, turning instead to the facilitation of inquiry, Dewey expresses unease with his own language of philosophy's unveiling of the "meanings" of the mass of facts accumulated by the full gamut of human investigations. Directing philosophy toward counseling various types of inquiry provides a familiar, and credible, task. It is, nonetheless a retreat from James's own ambitious hope—to help people to better versions of whatever chaotic and inchoate vision of the world and their place in it guides their aspirations and activities.

The difficulty of taking that task seriously lies in recognizing temptation: the seductive power of grandiosity. What the confused hat-wearer appears to need is a full perspective on everything, a "world-formula," or an understanding of the "meanings" of all the information available from the current state of inquiries in all domains, or Sellars's broad perspective on "things" and their "hanging together." What many commentators describe—in a usage that typically irritates philosophers—as "someone's philosophy." The philosophical wince stems from a commendable modesty. If finding a world-formula, a grand overarching perspective, is to be the philosophical enterprise, it is almost certainly grandiose, overweening, "vaulting ambition." Surely anything offered along these lines will be superficial—and probably banal?

So, as I read him, Dewey backs off. He urges philosophers to survey all the various domains in which inquiry is pursued, more or less successfully. The task is to reflect on them, to refine the methods of those that are plainly making progress, and to develop new tools for the ones that currently struggle. Dewey's recommendation is a far broader version of Hempel's proposal for logical empiricist philosophy of science. Hempel wanted to address questions arising for the various sciences, hoping to refine the methods of the flourishing ones and nurture those in their infancy. Dewey recognizes, insightfully, that inquiry goes on in all manner of contexts and all kinds of domains, and refuses to limit the search for method to the ventures we label as "scientific." In particular, he sees the principal challenge as developing methods for moral, ethical, social, and political forms of inquiry (Dewey 1909/1998).

Dewey's generalization specifies *part* of what—borrowing a term from my accusers—I'll call *core philosophy*. Unlike the search for a universal perspective on the world in which we live and on the possibilities for human lives, it doesn't appear entirely hopeless, doomed to failure or to shallow pseudo-success. After all, people have succeeded at this kind of work. They reflect on the kinds of procedures that have led to progress in some chosen domain, take note of the ways in which advances have been blocked, and try to provide a systematic account of how future investigations might better be conducted. They may be aided by comparisons with other domains, perhaps especially those whose successes seem most striking. In effect, people who attempt to do philosophy in this way are practicing *modus Cartwright* in different places, and sometimes on a broader scale.

Yet to take these Deweyan projects as the whole of core philosophy would shrink the enterprise James envisages. For there are many aspects of everyday experience besides human inquiry. Although I think *Homo quaerens* is a better name for our species than the one assigned by biological taxonomy—*sapiens* is far too self-congratulatory, and even *cognoscens* would be overdoing it—all kinds of situations and conditions figure in the experience of ordinary folk, generating chaos and confusion under a vast number of hats. People need tools for making sense of their individual experiences, to determine for themselves their own identities and central aspirations, to formulate and refine and revise their "plans of life," and to decide where and about what to inquire. Can philosophy respond to their needs, without taking on the impossible burden of supplying "world-formulas"?

I believe that it can. For a very simple reason. Sometimes it has.

***

The world we inhabit often seems far more complicated than the ones in which the great philosophers of the past made their wide-ranging proposals. Should that excuse contemporary philosophers from pursuing synthetic philosophy? Aristotle could do it. Kant, perhaps, could do it. Sadly, though, we can't do it.

To be sure, nobody today can hope to write as intelligently on so many topics as Aristotle did. Yet it's worth asking: did Aristotle write about *everything* that mattered to his contemporaries? Certainly not. He ignored a fair number of areas of potential concern to various groups of people—most evidently, the slaves and the women of his age. Even if we restrict attention to the well-born male members of the polis, did he provide them with a complete account of how everything hangs together? His works are a serious candidate for "most impressive synthesis of current knowledge ever given." But they are silent, or scanty in what they say, on any number of issues: questions about religion, economic life, education, and the treatment of animals, for example. Is the synthesis only incomplete because the pertinent texts—like the examination of comedy—have gone missing?

Kant is the only subsequent philosopher whose synthetic scope might rival Aristotle's. Scholars routinely praise the depth and intricacy of his analyses and arguments, but, to my mind, the *breadth* of his knowledge is equally breathtaking. Even Kant, however, didn't cover *everything*. Like some twentieth-century philosophers, his understanding of the sciences was shaped by a few parts of physics. Less at home with chemistry, as it was developing during the 1780s, he appears to have had little interest in theories about the history of the Earth, in the mathematical analysis developed by Euler and Lagrange, or in eighteenth-century political economy. Like Frege, I have "no wish to incur the reproach of picking petty quarrels with a genius to whom we must all look up with grateful awe" (Frege 1884/1968, 101ᵉ). The point is simple (and, I hope, uncontroversial). Some dead philosophers have systematized large and important parts of what was known when they wrote. Nobody has ever achieved a grand, universal synthesis.

That should encourage those who write philosophy today. The complexity of the modern world may further limit the scope of contemporary efforts to provide a synthetic picture from which a significant portion of the human population might draw—as, for example, German youth once drew from Kant, and a later generation drew from Schopenhauer. Maybe ours have to be on a smaller scale. Nevertheless, *partial* syntheses, attempts to make sense of some cluster of phenomena, can serve the purpose toward which James's remark about world-formulas points. Especially when they respond to a kind of confusion or some localized chaos that affects a sizeable group of people.

The encouragement is fortified by reflecting on other contributors to the Western philosophical canon, thinkers whose syntheses were plainly narrower than those of Aristotle and Kant. Descartes is often taken to have revolutionized philosophy by instituting a search for absolute certainty—and thus provoking generations of epistemologists to take up a "core issue," the assessment (typically the attempted rebuttal) of skepticism about the external world. I view his achievements from a different angle. Inspired by the impending collapse of the Aristotelian synthesis in the early seventeenth century, Descartes drew from his own investigations of questions in mathematics and natural science—geometry, optics, and meteorology—a method whose use, he believed, would help his contemporaries build a substitute for the previous orthodoxy. Concern aroused by the two-thousand-year dominance of a faulty framework led him to impose a stringent demand on his method: it must be guaranteed not to lead us astray. Thus arose his quest for certainty. It was a spin-off from a commitment to replacing a (decrepit) synthesis. Regarded in this way, the supposed "core issue" is a secondary question, one caused by Descartes's (understandable) sense of appalling error—he saw people as having been beguiled for two millennia. Ironically, his aspiration not to make the mistake of his predecessor led him to commit a version of the same misstep. He started with an unscrutinized philosophical assumption: rebuilding has to be on immoveable foundations. His emphasis on the need for ironclad guarantees distorted epistemology for another two hundred (plus) years.

Or consider Schopenhauer. His magnum opus seems to be inspired by reflections on a familiar aspect of human experience: the satisfaction of desire is only temporary (Schopenhauer would have intensified the claim—it's evanescent). Combining this thought with his own reading of Kant, he suggested that the noumenal realm would be better characterized as the province of an insatiable will. The famous pessimism, so influential on fin-de-siècle German youth, developed from that conjunction of ideas. To those, like Thomas Mann, who felt the disappointment of evanescent relief from desire, Schopenhauer brought some order to the chaos of late adolescent, or early adult, ruminations.

Marx can also be viewed as a synthesizer, melding together ideas from Hegel and his successors, with a commitment to social reform and socialist ideals, all tempered by his own appraisal of the insights and oversights of classical political economy. The end result is an account of social and political life that attempts to make sense of its history, and to point the way to a genuinely scientific socialism.

Others, too. Kierkegaard struggled to make sense of the deep significance of religion and its debasement in his own times. Mill and Nietzsche, concerned in very different ways with the suppression of individualism, were determined to help to create a world in which individuals can develop and flourish. William James, driven by a desire to honor science and oppose scientism, found a place for religion and for the deepening of values in a world that threatened to eliminate what he regarded as most important in human life. John Dewey, playing fox to James's hedgehog, surveyed many difficulties in the society he knew best: recognizing the shortcomings of existing educational practices in their distortion of young people's growth, diagnosing the limitations of democratic institutions, trying to find ways of bringing art back into the everyday lives of his fellow citizens, seeking a conception of religion that could preserve what is valuable while abandoning superstition.

I have been engaging in a quick exercise of *modus Cartwright.* "Here are some philosophers: try thinking of them this way." I've proposed viewing my exemplars (and I could add many more) as forming partial syntheses to account for widespread features of human experience. They had an influence on others, sometimes immediately, sometimes much later, because they supposed significant groups of people would share their puzzlement about the facets of human life to which they tried to bring order. And they were right about that.

Yet, in one obvious respect, I must acknowledge the historical distortion I have committed. For most of them would have regarded their synthesis as a cognitive achievement. Not simply a proposal for straightening things out, but as declaring to the world how matters, in their chosen domain, *should* be straightened out. That, I suggest, mischaracterizes what they actually achieved. They should have maintained the modesty of *modus Cartwright*. Here are some phenomena: *try* thinking about them in this way.

***

Contemporary philosophy could emulate these synthesizing efforts. Indeed, it sometimes does. Our own times are not entirely bereft of ventures in the same vein. Recent English-language philosophy has offered some attempts to make coherent sense of aspects of the world in which we live.

Twentieth-century paradigms of synthetic work are visible in Kuhn's studies of scientific change and in Rawls's explorations of justice and of political liberalism (Kuhn 1962; Rawls 1999, 1993). Both authors offer the broader world large pictures of areas of human existence that concern significant numbers of people. Kuhn's is narrower and more specialized, intended to reshape prior understanding of the sciences and their development, their past contributions and their potential achievements. Rawls presses closer to the everyday concerns of the citizen, aiming to bring some order to the chaos and confusion boiling away under people's hats when they try to wrestle with questions about the justice of laws and institutions, or to determine the proper limits on political freedoms.

As I read them, both are practicing *modus Cartwright*. Each has read widely. Their work is grounded in facts uncovered by first-order investigators (from several disciplines), and sometimes involves reflection on their own experiences. Kuhn assembles information from the history of the sciences (and from other parts of history), from psychology and from sociology, and from his own struggles in coming to terms with the discarded perspectives of the past. Rawls ranges even more broadly, drawing on ethics and political theory, on economics, on the history of political life, and on an understanding of the sources of human motivations drawn both from a wide reading and from unusual powers of sympathy. Out of these sources they gather a body of phenomena to be brought into order. Their great achievements lie in articulating a way of viewing these phenomena. "Try looking at this part of life from this angle," they suggest.

What brings them an audience is their initial success in circumscribing a domain in which nonphilosophers (even people of no great education) seek guidance. And then in offering something to readers who previously "didn't know their way about" in an area of interest or concern to them. Their writings satisfy a genuine need rather than "filling a welcome gap in the literature."

I have selected my examples deliberately, to avoid arousing too much of the common suspicion of larger synthetic ventures in philosophy. I hope not to provoke the kinds of grumbles often heard in response to James's talk of "world-formulas" and kindred declarations. Even philosophers who disagree sharply with Rawls's conclusions find it hard to denigrate his work, or to resist conceding its stature in the history of political thought. Kuhn, by contrast, has sometimes been the target of harsh criticism, accused of being philosophically insensitive and not fully understanding the details of the issues about which he attempted (allegedly inadequately) to deal. In the early decades after the publication of his study of scientific revolutions, he was routinely lumped with Feyerabend as one of the "leaders of the new fuzzies" and lambasted for his supposed "relativism." Although the tone of the complaints is milder today, some of the substance endures.

Is high-quality synthetic philosophy a thing of the past (if only of the relatively recent past)? I think not. It endures today in the writings of some creative and insightful philosophers. To illustrate, I shall point to six exemplars (paradigms?), recognizing that others might opt for different lists: Elizabeth Anderson (Anderson 2010, 2017), Anthony Appiah (Appiah 1992, 2006, 2018), Nancy Cartwright (1983, 1999, 2007, 2019), Alexander Nehamas (1998, 2007, 2016), Susan Neiman (2002, 2008, 2014, 2019), and Martha Nussbaum (2011, 2012, 2015, 2016). Although I would not advertise my list as complete, I think these exemplars are much rarer than they should be. As I shall suggest in the following chapter, each might inspire young philosophers who have felt the concerns previous chapters have aired.

Each of these authors focuses on some aspects of the contemporary world that raise questions or perplexities for a sizeable group of people. James might view them as responding to different sources of subhat chaos. Anderson, for example, writes insightfully about how people from different races (with a tortured history of oppression, suffering, and mistrust) might come to live together in mutually satisfying ways, and about the unobserved channels through which our lives are shaped. Appiah develops sophisticated accounts of identities, with particular attention to individuals who are often seen in the light of one, or several, stereotypes, and he explores the possibilities of genuine community. Nehamas is concerned with the place of beauty in the modern world, with the lifelong search for beauty, and the ancient question of the good life. Neiman's synthetic endeavor stems from a conviction that concern with evil lies at the heart of modern thought, and she examines the forms in which evil arises and the strategies deployed to combat it. Nussbaum's many wide-ranging studies include presentations of an original and influential way of thinking about the quality of human lives, explorations of the role of the emotions in politics, proposals for facilitating the development of marginalized groups, and defenses of the importance of liberal education. (In each case, I have considered only a selection of the topics and themes these philosophers explore.)

Like Rawls and Kuhn, these philosophers, too, practice *modus Cartwright*. They gather diverse phenomena, identified by first-order investigators. They try to bring order to the phenomena, resolving tensions and increasing coherence. They offer a perspective to help those who are conscious of specific areas of subcranial chaos.

Despite their ability to reach readers beyond philosophy, like Kuhn, each of those I have listed is sometimes the target of professional suspicion, and even dismissal, with the frequency and the intensity of condemnation varying from case to case. Sometimes, it seems, success in having an impact on a wider world automatically elicits the disdainful sniffs of "real philosophers." Even people whom I greatly admire have complained that an attempt to bring order to some domain of everyday confusions, even one I view as exemplary, is "philosophically shallow" or that some part of it "isn't up with the recent literature on the topic." The first dismissal arises from the correct perception that the analyses on offer are not pursued as far as professional philosophers, writing for one another, would take them. Notions or principles are introduced without attempting to make them cover all possible cases. Here the disdainful critic is in the grip of the fetish of complete clarity. The appropriate question to ask is a different one. Has the principle or concept been sufficiently clarified to satisfy the needs of the groups whose perplexities are to be addressed? Is it readily applicable in the instances where interested readers would like to apply it? Those are the questions that matter. Sometimes, to be sure, ventures in synthetic philosophy are flawed. Overreach produces superficiality. The brush used in painting the picture is too broad. That judgment is, I believe, unwarranted in the examples I have offered. Moreover, to concede the possibility that attempts at synthesis will be flawed is not to justify a hair-trigger reaction, to see the ability to speak to a wider audience as guaranteeing the author's desertion of "real philosophy." What the fetishist proposes is a "professional rewriting" that would not only be unnecessary but would also interfere with the comprehension of the intended readership. Sufficient unto the public is the clarity of the synthesis!

The second charge can be dismissed more briefly. Professional philosophers may be irritated that a discussion neglects "the recent literature." Before they give in to that irritation, they should ask themselves two questions. First, would the synthesis do a better job for the intended audience if the author had absorbed the analytic studies the critic has in mind? Second, the synthesizers I admire are neither lazy nor illiterate. They read widely about their phenomena, exploring many different perspectives. Would their time have been better spent combing the specialized books and journals so that they would be thoroughly up on the most recent wrinkles? I suspect that these authors do glance at the "journal literature" from time to time. Perhaps their response when they do so is akin to mine: Not much here to help with what I am trying to do.

Do the knee-jerk reactions of contemporary professionals stem from an impulse pervading the history of Western philosophy? Ever since Plato, major thinkers have distrusted good writing. Yet, even if the language of the poets is unsuited to philosophical clarity and precision, Plato himself surely demonstrated to his successors that philosophy does not have to be esoteric or turgid, that it may be accessible, and that "loose" is not an inevitable adjective to accompany "popular" in application to philosophy. True enough, authors whose sense of style inclines to variation in phraseology may introduce ambiguities by presenting the same idea in different guises—William James is sometimes led into this temptation (and pays the price for his sin). Throughout much of the history of philosophy, to be sure, the stylistic expectations of readers were sufficiently low to allow many influential thinkers to nourish a large class of consumers with oatmeal prose. (Although Plato, Augustine, Descartes, Hume, Schopenhauer, Mill, Kierkegaard, Nietzsche, James, and Russell constitute a sizeable cohort of eminently readable exceptions.) Today's readers, however, have become adjusted to a spicier diet. So the insistence on "plain language" would seem to be a recipe for an esoteric future.

Complaints about the "superficiality" or "unphilosophical character" of attempts at synthetic philosophy, whether justified or not, arise with different frequencies for different authors. I incline to a testable hypothesis: The number of dismissive objections varies directly with the perceived size of the synthetic philosopher's audience. Perhaps that points to a seventh pathology: the urge to deter fellow philosophers from discharging the whole function of philosophy.

***

My sympathy for work in the history of philosophy should now start to appear more comprehensible. When I was a graduate student, historians of philosophy were often regarded as second-class citizens. In the intervening decades, things have changed for the better. The careful scholarship that has been done, on the Ancients, on Hume and Kant, on Hegel and Nietzsche, and on many others has proven valuable for the fledgling synthetic efforts of our day. We return to the ambitious synthesizers of the past— in part because so little in present philosophy answers to the task they undertook, in part because some of their concepts and questions continue to seem relevant today. For history to play this valuable role, the historian must chart a careful course, avoiding any tendency to wrench the text to current philosophical fashions (reading the great figures of the past as groping precursors of our most enlightened contemporaries). I confess to committing the latter type of error in some of my own historical work—but that doesn't interfere with my admiration for studies that consider past philosophers in their contexts, taking them on their own terms and still revealing ideas that speak to us.

Let me sum up. Philosophers can do valuable work in clarifying and advancing the debates that arise in various individual domains of human life, and in supplying synthetic perspectives to help people with the perplexities generated when they think about the world in which they live and about their own place in it. The past decade has witnessed an encouraging trend: more work of this kind is being done. Yet the vision of professional philosophers is often constricted in comparison with the giants of the past. Today, there are vast numbers of well-trained people, even graduate students, whose analytic skills, powers of dissecting arguments, exceed those of the great figures in the history of philosophy. That is, of course, a good thing. Clarity is a philosophical virtue. (Even if it is not the *only* philosophical virtue.) Attempts at synthesis made by people who lack the training, who do not think or write precisely, however popular they may be, are worthless—that is the correct insight behind the dismissive complaints. Nonetheless, some of those who try to renew the synthetic enterprise of philosophy's past, including those I have selected as exemplars, have been properly schooled. They retain the techniques instilled by the études of their graduate school years. Now, they want to make music—new sonatas and suites and concertos. And many outsiders listen and appreciate.

Because the world in which we live grows ever more complicated, the syntheses individual philosophers accomplish are likely
to be smaller than those attempted by the historical figures who
excite our admiration and who reward our rereading (for all their
relative lack of analytic training!). Future philosophy may, however, take advantage of an opportunity to imitate other areas of
investigation, in which progress is promoted through a division of
labor. Perhaps, in the future, teams of philosophers will collaborate on synthetic work in adjacent areas, striving collectively for an
overall perspective sufficiently broad to match some of the efforts
of our philosophical predecessors. Even if that occurs, I hope
there will always be room for individual voices—for, as we shall
see, philosophical progress depends on the richness of the varied
proposals the philosophical community offers.

Synthetic philosophy hopes to revive the past embedding of
ideas in human lives. Before philosophy was thoroughly professionalized, the writings of figures like Kant, Hegel, Schopenhauer,
Mill, Marx, and Nietzsche were devoured by large numbers of
people who didn't think of themselves as philosophers. Those people were hungry. They had a genuine need for systematic thinking.
If people trained in philosophy don't do it, it may be done partially
and implicitly—often helpfully—by artists and scholars in other
fields. Cavell and those he has inspired have done valuable work
in serving as "liaison officers" between literary works (and movies
and pieces of music) and philosophy's often underfed audiences.
Unfortunately, the appetites of those audiences are sometimes
sated by writers who have neither the skills of the artist in evoking
a philosophical perspective, nor the analytic training to present it
explicitly, by writing with precision and clarity. The professionals

are correct to view *some* grand synthetic efforts as amateurish and grandiose. Where they err is in supposing that *any* attempt to respond to public hunger should be automatically dismissed.

You don't need to believe in a comprehensive world-formula, some philosophical analog of Newton's dream for a fully unified science, to take up the synthetic venture. You need simply to recognize the wisdom expressed by Margaret Wilcox, the protagonist of E. M. Forster's *Howards End*: Only connect.

***

My discussion so far has definitely not supplied an account of synthetic philosophy sufficient to enable readers to classify any possible instance of philosophical writing. I hope, however, it has been clear enough to enable people attracted to this kind of work to envisage how they might undertake it. Perhaps, though, they might be aided by a brief account of how one of my own attempts at this genre originated and was developed.

Provoked by Dewey's heterodox suggestion that philosophy was centrally concerned with education, I began, some years ago, to read in this (often-despised) area of philosophy. I quickly discovered the contempt often directed toward the field to be entirely undeserved. During the past decades, a number of philosophers have done work on education that is both of high intellectual quality and socially relevant. Nonetheless, I found myself raising questions about the correctness of the assumptions normally framing discussions of education. A newcomer to the field, as I was, encounters any number of proposals about what education ought to do and how the proper purposes should be achieved.

Those proposals are typically made specific by supposing certain kinds of institutions—schools, universities, a fixed period during which education begins and ends—to be parts of the framework, within which the details are to be worked out. Turning to the history of education, I was struck by the accidents that develop those institutions in particular ways: the emphasis on good citizenship spurred by events that bring home the need for solidarity and community, the increased focus on science when it seems that a rival nation achieves a technological breakthrough (as in the launching of Sputnik). Moreover, the institutions themselves were once founded to serve very different functions from the ones people currently endorse: schools were originally inspired by the need to have scribes; higher education as a set of general studies entered universities that had previously been devoted to one of the professions—medicine, law, and theology—only as a necessary preliminary for candidates who were poorly prepared.

The classic philosophical writings on education, those of Plato and Rousseau and Mill, for example, provoked a question: How on earth can anyone expect to instill all the knowledge, skills, and character traits the philosophers want young adults to acquire? Conceiving the issue from the viewpoint of the individual, generations of philosophers have found all kinds of plausible ideals for the well-educated person, and they have proposed curricula to suit the goals they take to be most crucial. In some philosophical writings, appreciation for the attractions of many ideals is expressed in the problem of overload. So many desiderata, so much to learn! Hence, on occasion, the curriculum becomes so vast as to appear ludicrous—nobody, it seems, could manage to absorb it all without a decades-long commitment. In practice, of course, representatives of the state decide on a selection. There is, then, a shift from thinking of what would be good for the individual pupil to considering what the state most needs. In the modern world this is keyed to the interest in economic and technological success. Reflections on how to shape good citizens, or to prepare people to live fulfilling lives, take second place—if they come in at all. As talented historians have shown (Graham 2005), American education (and education in other affluent democracies) has tended to lurch from one set of central purposes to another, driven by the perceived needs of a society at various times. The emphasis on the imperative to outproduce and outcompete rival nations is simply the latest chapter in this disjointed story.

Parents all over the world hope the schools their children attend will help them develop, to be the best they can be. How those parents think about what is best is inevitably shaped by a large variety of factors, some drawn from the dominant culture ("Our daughter needs to learn how to support herself"), some from their own relation to other institutions ("It's important that she keeps her faith and forms a firm moral compass"), some from their sense of what has been important (or lost) in their own lives ("I would hate her to lose her freedom and spontaneity"), some from their social and political commitments ("She needs to understand the importance of community and serving the community"). They, too, are overloaded, wanting many things for their kids, and not seeing clearly how to come to a manageable selection.

These, then, were some of my phenomena. Chaotic and confused. My task was to bring them to order. Not just for myself. I was convinced that perplexities about what counts as good education were widely shared. And in that, if in nothing else, I quickly found out that I was correct.

An invitation to give a series of three lectures inspired me to draft some preliminary thoughts on these topics. I offered an overview of what I took to be the central predicament (the problem of overload), presented ideas about education for democratic citizenship, and considered the role of the sciences and the arts in education. My audience surely had a small minority of philosophers (the lectures were "in the Humanities"), possibly a majority of students and faculty, but it also contained a significant number of people from outside the academy. The discussion convinced me of two things: first that I had touched a nerve—many people were interested in these questions (however skeptical they were about my answers); secondly that I had a considerable way to go. Three and a bit years later, my attempts to respond to the many points my audience raised has appeared as a longish book (Kitcher 2021b).

My aim in these paragraphs isn't to advertise, but to use my own experience to make more vivid how an enterprise in synthetic philosophy might take root and grow. In this case, the starting point is an accident. A surprising sentence of Dewey's inspired me to look at a facet of human life of which I had direct experience (my own schooling), vicarious experience (the education of my children), and on which I had sometimes engaged in confused reflections. I supposed, from the beginning, that education is important in the lives of many people, and that my own uncertainties and perplexities would be widely shared—judgments that were later confirmed. So I attempted a synthetic project, rounding up phenomena from various sources, and trying to make sense of the whole. Bringing some order to the chaos under my own hat and offering the result to others.

One feature of this example may suggest good places in which to look for the starting points from which synthetic philosophy can grow. Our lives are wholes, but we live them in and across many domains: we work and we play, we teach and are educated, we earn money and we spend it, we play sports and we pursue other hobbies, we participate in political life and we worship (or turn our backs on religion), we form friendships and (sometimes) provoke enmity, we fall in love. The domains are inhabited by conventions, norms, rules, roles, and institutions. Each individual domain may make what is, by its own lights, progress: the church may be renewed, the economic system may become more efficient, love may be deepened and enriched, or the recognition of loving relations may be broadened.

Yet it is possible, it seems, that progress in some domains may inhibit the progressive development of others. There can be *institutional friction*. That occurs when a change occurring in one set of institutions counts, according to the standards reigning in that domain as an advance, but also imposes checks on the progress of another domain. The apparently progressive domain constrains its neighbor, preventing advances or, worse, even causing regress. That occurs in the example I have given. Economic life constrains practices of education. The priority given to the goal of self-maintenance ("getting a good job") crowds out other educational values—finding a satisfying identity, preparation for a fulfilling life, becoming a good citizen—because the apparent streamlining of economic arrangements demands more time for the development of work-related skills, at cost to less "practical" studies.

It would be foolish to suppose the only source of widespread perplexity to be those points at which institutional friction occurs. For the aspiring synthetic philosopher, however, I suggest these as good places to look.

***

My attempt to characterize synthetic philosophy intentionally falls short of complete clarity. Those who demand a criterion enabling them to occupy the judgment seat and divide all works of philosophy into two classes, the significant sheep and the game-playing goats, will be doomed to disappointment. The more serious charge is that I have not said enough to settle live doubts about particular projects concerned philosophers have undertaken or are considering for themselves. Are the concepts I have introduced too vague and indefinite to enable the self-examination I have urged on the profession of philosophy?

It would be contrary to the spirit of this book for me to legislate—*nobody* should claim the throne, canonizing some and dismissing others to perdition. The notions of synthetic philosophy, of contributions to inquiry (broadly construed), of philosophy that bears on the issues of the day, together with the resulting distinction between "those disputes that collapse into insignificance" and those that are genuinely worthwhile, have been characterized discursively and illustrated by example. I have rounded up some phenomena, labeling them either as instances of a concept or as cases to which it does not apply. Those provide tools for self-questioning. Reflective philosophers may want to discard some of them and apply others. The decision about what is, and what is not, worth pursuing should not be forced upon them from an external standpoint. Each of us ought to look at our lives from a number of angles, comparing what we conceive of doing with the "experiments of living" pursued by others, and considering whether the pattern of similarities and differences corresponds to our own sense of spending our existence wisely. In a world where it is all too easy for highly talented people to adopt the conventions of a profession with obvious attractions, what is crucial is to undermine complacency, to suggest angles from which everyday practices look less obviously important, and to *initiate* a process of self-interrogation. I hope I have said enough to start that— philosophical—trial and to provide some resources for conducting it appropriately. The eventual verdict, however, must be your own.

***

Like the philosophers whose synthetic work I commended earlier, I have been trying to employ *modus Cartwright*. As you may have observed, in my overly brief accounts of their enterprises one of my paradigms was absent—the philosopher whose name I have attached to that style of argument. In fact, Nancy Cartwright is doubly exemplary for my purposes in this book. For her work divides into two main genres. Writing generally about science, she offers a new perspective on how we should think about the scientific enterprise. Parts of that perspective have become widely accepted, not only through her writings but because of contributions by other members of the "Stanford school" (notably John Dupré). Here she is doing synthetic philosophy with respect to a specific domain, the area we think of as scientific practice. At other times, her studies are directed toward the ways in which particular pieces of science are used in developing policies with social impact. That part of her work falls under the so-called peripheral ventures I praised in the first chapter. Some of the time, then, she is doing synthetic philosophy, and at other times she is using ("applying"?) philosophy to make a direct contribution to specific (and urgent) social problems.

Which of these genres is more important? I find the question impossible to answer. What criterion would we appeal to in rating one kind as more important—more "central to philosophy" than the other? Nor do I believe in a sharp distinction between them. For, if the synthesis is relatively small-scale and the social problem relatively broad, either label may be appropriate. The boundary between "two genres" becomes indecipherable. An exploration of the potential ethical losses faced by people who aspire to a very different kind of life than the ones common in the communities into which they are born (the "strivers" as Jennifer Morton calls them in an insightful recent book) can be viewed either as addressed to a single social problem or as presenting a synthetic perspective on a class of issues highly significant to anyone whose chosen plan of life involves a disruption of community. The label attached to studies like this is unimportant. If they are pursued with the care and sensitivity of Morton (2020), their value is evident.

So, although I have used a ladder to climb, I now want to kick it away. My articulation of James's conception of "the whole function of philosophy" was an attempt to embrace an insight of critics of my earlier efforts to offer a pragmatist account of philosophy.

They saw me, rightly, as missing something. They called it *core philosophy*, and I went along with that language. It was a convenience for starting a debate about what the core might contain. Champions of today's professionalized philosophy will think of it as containing some selection from analytic metaphysics, analytic epistemology, analytic philosophy of mind, and analytic philosophy of language. I have proposed to empty the core of those ventures and fill it with different things: the search for methods of inquiry in various first-order fields of investigation, and synthetic philosophy, probably on smaller scales than in earlier historical periods. That proposal is now conjoined with my earlier endorsement of philosophical attempts to respond to urgent problems. Does that make a piebald core and a monochrome periphery? Do I still want to turn philosophy inside out?

These are silly questions, artifacts of a linguistic decision, one useful for focusing my response to an important critical insight. Having reached a tripartite explanation of philosophical value, we no longer need a core-periphery distinction. Instead, there are three kinds of valuable philosophy: the Deweyan methodological project, synthetic philosophy, and philosophical attempts to help with urgent problems. Maybe some more—I cannot reasonably claim completeness. But any additions should make some difference to the lives of some significant number of people, somehow, somewhere, and somewhen. The professionals' core is unlikely, I think, to meet that test.

So a provisional answer to the question posed in the title of this book. Philosophy has its uses. Important uses. Three of them. To help resolve the problems and debates of the age; to offer tools for various branches of inquiry; and to provide perspectives, synthetic responses to the chaos under people's hair (if not their hats).

***

But what exactly does it give to the intellectual and social worlds? I want to close by trying for a little further clarity and precision. We can make some progress on this issue by reflecting on a recent debate, centered on the question of philosophy's progress.

This is, I believe, typically couched in the wrong terms. Philosophy is taken to strive for theories, and the theories are intended to be true. But philosophers always disagree, and the disagreements persist—indeed, they are so long-lasting, and so much ingenuity is displayed in conducting them, that it would be folly to hail any philosophical theory as true. Hence pessimism: there is no progress in philosophy.

For some people, including powerful outsiders (perhaps a Provost or Dean, keen on translational research and impatient with the interminable debates endemic to supposedly important disciplines), there's a corollary. In hard budgetary times, you can cut, or even abolish, the philosophy department. Why invest in researchers who never offer any new knowledge? My answer is straightforward: because, working in the interstices of the fields of first-order inquiry, philosophy helps all those fields and helps humanity to take full advantage of their epistemic achievements. It does so by offering cognitive resources—not theories of everything (or, indeed, anything) but concepts, questions, suggestive arguments, and analogies. Those are useful in individual deliberations as people try to come to terms with the particular muddles that lie under their hats, in collective deliberations as we engage with one another in trying to work through the ethical, social, and political issues of our times, in the pursuit of all those important styles of investigation (including the ones my tough-minded administrator favors most). To adapt a phrase from James, the trail of the philosophical serpent is over it all.

Of course, ventures in synthetic philosophy are often full of propositions—or, better, proposals. Does the value of the synthesis turn on whether they are correct? Surely not. Philosophy changes the way people think, the way they see the world, by accomplishing a change of perspective. Experience is conceptualized differently. New possibilities come into view. Connections are made between aspects of life that were once "loose and separate." The audience is invited to pursue a certain line of reasoning. Questions emerge that had not been posed before. The proposals are best seen as signposts, pointing to changes of Gestalt.

Why do we continue to read the great philosophers of the past? Not, I suggest, because we take them to have offered a true theory, but because of the other things they provide. The argument of the *Euthyphro* (and Kant's deepening of it) is relevant to contemporary discussions of moral questions that confront us; the Aristotelian ideal of friendship helps us to pose questions about relationships on the internet; the concepts of "the state of nature" and "the social contract" are alive in our political discussions; so, too, are Mill's conception of liberalism and Rawls's notion of the original position; the retrospective test for the value of a life, posed by Schopenhauer and elaborated by Nietzsche, is one consideration thoughtful people employ in trying to figure out what kind of person they should be; talk of paradigms is everywhere (even though Kuhn wanted to take back the word).

One of the great insights behind Kuhn's seminal monograph, one appreciated by the many practicing scientists who have read it with pleasure, is its recognition of the multidimensionality of scientific practice. The science of a time is not adequately characterized as a collection of propositions. As Kuhn saw, and as many philosophers of science have argued since, it is distinguished by its concepts, its questions, its standards, its methodological rules, its preferred modes of reasoning, its tools and techniques—as well as the answers it gives to the questions it has picked out as significant.

We ought to think of other areas of life as Kuhn invited us to think about the sciences. Individuals and communities engage in multidimensional practices in their work and their play, in their friendships and enmities, in their politics and their religions, in their educations and their lawmaking. They adopt a certain language, commend various forms of action, endorse certain kinds of reasoning, and are motivated by some analogies and not others. All of that is subject to change. Philosophy can prompt and lead the change, not by delivering new accepted truths, but at a more fundamental level.

We should think of philosophy as guiding human practices through its achievements in introducing concepts, proposing lines of reasoning, suggesting standards and rules, posing questions, offering striking comparisons, opening up possibilities, and so on. From that perspective, the enduring fascination of texts written centuries, or millennia, ago becomes readily comprehensible. When, as it happens, a philosopher puts forward a proposition widely accepted as true, it is likely to become someone else's property, taken over by scientists or mathematicians or political theorists or medical ethicists. Those people develop it further, and, after a while, the philosophical origins are forgotten.

The progress of philosophy doesn't stand or fall according to whether the would-be synthesizer arrives at a true overarching theory. The crucial question is different: Do the efforts at synthesis generate resources that prove useful, whether for some systematic field of inquiry, or for collective efforts to resolve difficult questions, or for people's attempts to make sense of their lives? I see the long history of Western philosophy as providing a resoundingly positive answer to this question. A century's worth of work in which Anglophone philosophers have largely turned away from synthetic ambitions makes that answer far less convincing today. Indeed, the unconvinced are everywhere—as with my Thatcherite administrator whose hatchet reforms the university.

Skepticism about the value of philosophy is not only damaging when research universities trim their philosophy faculty. It is just as bad, maybe worse, when philosophy declines or vanishes from *any* educational setting—when community college students don't have access to philosophy courses, when there is no longer a major at the liberal arts college, when high schools think of the philosophy club as dispensable, when programs to bring philosophy into the prisons or into the lives of ex-prisoners are no longer encouraged. For, as those things disappear, large groups of people lose the opportunity, not only to think more clearly but also to reflect upon and challenge their inherited ways of viewing the world. The philosophical milieu in which I grew up passed on a narrow view of philosophical success. I want to celebrate all those who have done very much what James commended, the teachers at all levels who have trained people to use philosophical tools in tidying up the chaos of what they carry about under their hats. In doing so, they have helped fulfill "the whole function of philosophy." I'm not sure I can say as much.

***

I've pointed to a pragmatic argument for contemporary philosophers to show how they can contribute something more than clever solutions to puzzles of interest only to a privileged coterie. In hard times, administrators will ponder the value of paying people to continue what they see as an ingrown conversation. The line of thought I've developed from James and Dewey offers a more philosophical, albeit pragmatist, alternative: We should see our lives as making a positive difference to a project larger than ourselves, and so renew the grand—synthetic—tradition of Western philosophy. Thus it is appropriate for us to reflect periodically on the worth of the work we are doing, on whether it makes a difference, and, if so, how. In Chapter 1, I tried to assess the current state of Anglophone philosophy, by focusing on direct connections with particular domains of inquiry or on urgent social issues. That is one way for philosophers to make differences, but it is not the only one. As I have suggested in this chapter, James's apparently strange talk of "world-formulas" can be elaborated, with a little help from Dewey, to identify a different species of linkage, one to whose value the history of our discipline proudly testifies.

It should go without saying that my conclusions should be debated, possibly revised, or even discarded entirely. More than half a century ago, I left mathematics because I didn't want to devote my life to solving intricate problems. I entered philosophy sideways, and that may have distorted my vision. Even so, as the history of philosophy reveals so clearly, sometimes a provocative falsehood stimulates fruitful discussions and leads to increased self-awareness. It can be a stepping-stone to greater self-understanding and to the fashioning of helpful cognitive resources.

In our best moments, when we reflect upon our lives, most of us want to make a positive difference to the world into which we have come and which we shall ultimately leave. We hope that what we have done with our lives will have left it better than we have found it, albeit almost certainly in tiny ways. Mill concluded his Inaugural Address as rector of St Andrews University, by exhorting each of the (male) undergraduates who had elected him "to leave his fellow creatures some little better for the use he has known how to make of his intellect." Dewey rarely rises to the stylistic elegance of Mill's prose, but, toward the end of *A Common Faith*, he offers an eloquent elaboration of Mill's exhortation.

> We who now live are parts of a humanity that extends into the remote past, a humanity that has interacted with nature. The things in civilization we most prize are not of ourselves. They exist by grace of the doings and sufferings of the continuous human community in which we are a link. Ours is the responsibility of conserving, transmitting, rectifying and expanding the heritage of values we have received that those who come after us may receive it more solid and secure, more widely accessible and more generously shared than we have received it. (Dewey 1934/1986, 57–58)

Each of us is part of a multigenerational project, from which we borrow and to which we contribute. Even the most professional of professional Anglophone philosophers intends to advance the project. I have tried to make some proposals about how a philosophical career might do that.

Try thinking about a life devoted to philosophy this way.

5 | LETTER TO SOME YOUNG PHILOSOPHERS

I am extremely grateful to you for your questions and comments on two of the lectures from which my discussions here have been drawn. One of you asked the first question after I presented a version of Chapter 2 in 2017 at the meeting of the European Society for Philosophy of Science. Others have raised further questions after hearing (via Zoom) the John Dewey Lecture I delivered at the meeting of the Eastern Division of the American Philosophical Association in January 2021, either in the discussion following the lecture or in emails to me. A common theme runs through your queries and your comments: How can people at early stages of their careers take the risk of flouting the accepted standards of the profession they hope to join? As I said to that initial questioner, it's an important issue, and it deserves a full discussion. Although, in the past, I have tried to give answers, I'm sadly conscious of their inadequacy. Here, I shall try to do a bit better.

Apparently, some of the things I have said have resonated with you. You are sympathetic to a project for renewing philosophy. You, too, have felt dissatisfied with the game playing that often appears to be the be-all and end-all of professional philosophical lives. You do not wish to spend your own careers in this way. You would like to contribute to a broader philosophical project, one akin to what the past philosophers you admire most have pursued. You would like your work to have an impact on people's lives, beyond the philosophy profession and beyond the academy. Like me, you regret the dominant mood of judging such aspirations to be somehow second-rate, inferior to the supposedly important work that wins acceptance from "the top journals."

But you are young. Your careers are just beginning. You have no job security. Even if you are in a tenure-track position, you know that your chances of obtaining permanent employment will depend on assessments of your published work, perhaps of your work-in-progress, and that, at some stage of the process, your contributions will be assessed by people who adopt the dominant professional attitude. Although your colleagues may be sympathetic to the kind of philosophy you would like to write, it is highly likely that some of the external letters they solicit will be more dismissive. And, of course, your current post may be temporary, a postdoctoral fellowship, or a one-year "replacement" position. You may be scurrying from institution to institution as an underpaid adjunct. You may be struggling with a heavy teaching load, one those whose work enjoys high prestige would find intolerable. You may not even have a job at all.

So, you ask, what are you to do? You judge that, if you do not play by the rules, your prospects of continuing in philosophy are far from bright. Hence, however appealing you may find my call for reform, you see it as an invitation to gamble at unfavorable odds, where the loss would involve forfeiting the opportunities for which you have spent years of hard work preparing. It would be difficult to dispute your judgment. Also not to appreciate your tact. You have been too polite to point out that the invitation is issued by somebody who has retired, after decades of full job security, somebody who has nothing to lose.

Surely, then, I owe you a reply.

Before I take up your questions, a prefatory note seems in order. A few words of confession and apology. Although beginning a career in philosophy has never been easy (at least during the past half-century), I know the difficulties you experience today are more severe than at any time in the recent past. Jobs are scarce and the number of disappointed candidates seems to grow from year to year. I am also sure that there may be challenges of the current situation whose intensity I do not appreciate. Please forgive me if there are places in what follows where what I say seems tone-deaf.

I hope those passages won't occur too frequently. For my own career began in an unpromising fashion, with its own difficulties, and I am conscious of how its subsequent trajectory has been largely shaped by luck. Just over fifty years ago, I arrived at graduate school in Princeton, with virtually no philosophical training. Fortunately, although I was dismally unprepared for philosophy as Princeton then conceived it, a few people recognized some sparks of something and devoted themselves to knocking me into shape. My mentors were astute enough to view their crash course as incomplete and to steer me in the direction of an unfashionable dissertation topic, one they rightly perceived as suited to my background: I was to write on the historical search for a foundation for mathematics. Their advice has proven valuable, in ways nobody could have predicted at the time, in steering me to my own approach to philosophical questions. An approach totally unforeseen when I emerged from graduate school with an odd, but passable, dissertation.

The largest piece of luck entered my life with the arrival, in my second year of graduate education, of a young woman, then known as Patricia Williams. We have now been married a long time, both of us pursuing careers in philosophy. From the start, we were determined to avoid the "commuting marriages" we saw as undermining the unions of many academics. When I told my advisor of our resolution, he estimated the chances of our success, not by multiplying the independent probabilities of each of us finding a job, but as diminishing according to some nasty exponential decay function. That assessment was entirely rational. In those days, some colleges and universities had policies against hiring married couples in the same department. As, in a job interview, Pat was told by a member of a department that, some years later, appointed us both. In a moment when the prospects of working together appeared particularly bleak, black humor prompted us to canvass alternatives. Should we open a restaurant: *Kitcher and Kitcher Kurry with a 'K'*? (In those days, South Asian restaurants were relatively rare in the United States—and I was enjoying learning to cook what I then took to be Indian food.)

Most aspects of professional life in philosophy have become considerably worse in the decades since then. The opportunity for joint appointments isn't one of them. Prospects for married philosophers who hope to live in the same place are better than they were. Better, but far from perfect. I have been told that graduate students who live together and aim to find jobs in the same department have been warned "not to look at the Kitchers"—that's just "dumb luck."

We are saddened by the continued problems many philosophical couples still face. We had hoped that, by now, universities would have become more sympathetic to their predicaments and more imaginative in responding to them. Good fortune is still needed, and work remains to be done. Our own lives have certainly benefited from large doses of dumb luck.

So, if my replies to your questions sometimes appear to miss the deeper point, I hope you will excuse me. With some understanding of "where I am coming from."

I am not qualified to offer you advice, but, having observed people following various courses that might serve as options for you, I feel more confident presenting four models and reviewing their potential and their disadvantages. A small catalog of what Mill might have called "experiments of philosophizing." Although each possibility has been pursued by some people I know, people who have been satisfied with that specific choice, many of you, maybe most of you, are likely to find all of them inadequate, or, in the case of the last, unavailable to you. At the very least, then, more steps need to be taken to address your entirely justifiable aspirations. Senior members of the profession who sympathize with those hopes have a responsibility to consider the possibility of collective efforts in going forward, and I shall conclude with some tentative proposals.

My account in the preceding chapters concentrates on one part of a life in philosophy. I've been concerned with philosophical research, with the development of philosophy through the publication of books and articles, and the presentation of lectures to colleagues. But virtually no philosopher spends the entire working day in reading, writing, and talking to peers (at least, not before retirement). Almost every one of us teaches philosophy, bringing philosophical ideas and debates to people who, for the most part, never aspire to make their living in philosophy. That part of our job should not be viewed as a chore, something we're required to do in order to think through the issues that fascinate us. It is important, ought to be a vital part of a philosophical life, and should be informed by, and feed into, whatever creative philosophical work we do. Two of the options I shall consider emphasize this aspect of a philosophical career. Let's pause for a bit, then, and examine how the role of a philosophical teacher is developing and how it might help satisfy some of what you aspire to do.

If you follow James in thinking of philosophy as helping to sort out the chaos in people's conceptions of themselves and their lives, then the philosophy classroom is an obvious site at which this work can be accomplished. Drawing on all sorts of traditions, including the analytic philosophy of the last hundred years or so, teachers can provide their listeners with many tools for thinking more clearly, for conceptualizing the issues most important to them, for reshaping their tentative identities. The healthy impulses behind the pathologies can be cultivated, without prompting those who acquire them to indulge in the hypertrophied forms found among the professionals. Those you teach will go on to apply the skills in critical thinking you have instilled in them, in their careers and in their personal decisions. Their lives will go better for your instruction, and, perhaps, from time to time, they will recognize that and think of you with gratitude. Most of your audience leaves before addiction to any fetish starts.

Philosophers of my generation tend to think of this valuable instruction too narrowly. Your contemporaries are sometimes more imaginative. Several years ago, a few Columbia graduate students in philosophy combined with some of their peers at Teachers College, to begin a program of bringing philosophy into high schools. That enterprise has been enormously successful in helping young people, especially in places where the previous educational opportunities were slim. A later generation of graduate students has extended the venture to help people on parole (in the award-winning program *Rethink*). Some of my former colleagues have initiated further efforts, bringing philosophy to people in prison. Similar programs have been developed at other universities and have been equally fruitful. One of my great regrets is that this kind of work didn't emerge earlier, and that I haven't contributed to it.

Hence, I've talked about the philosophy teacher's "listeners" or "audience"—not necessarily to be centered on the paradigm of the undergraduate at an elite university or liberal arts college. Indeed, the *primary* places at which chaos begins to be reorganized may well be the community college, or the extension program, or the night classes, or the seminar for parolees, or the high school philosophy club, or the weekly prison discussion.

Teaching at these venues is typically under-respected and almost always underpaid (sometimes, even, unpaid). People engage in it because it enables them to identify, very clearly, the contributions they are making to the lives of others. Anyone who views lives as fulfilled when they make positive differences, small but by no means insignificant, to the multigenerational human project should celebrate these roles.

Option one for you is to put on that mantle and wear it proudly. Two former graduate students with whom I worked, one who completed a PhD, one who did not, decided on this as the best choice for them. Both were dedicated to philosophy—and equally dedicated to teaching precollege students. Finding themselves in a professional environment hostile to their own visions of what philosophy should do, they resolved not to force themselves into the molds expected of them but to teach under a regime in which their future writing would not be a factor in advancing, retarding, or ending their careers. They have retained the part of philosophical practice they love; they teach and enlighten young people, some of whom will go on to colleges and universities. In their spare time, these two devoted teachers can write the kinds of philosophy they value.

Would that satisfy you? Perhaps not. For you may reasonably fear that, without continued interactions with colleagues and with more advanced students, your own teaching would become more mechanical and less effective. Contrary to a popular stereotype, teaching and research are by no means incompatible. To be sure, there are only so many hours in a working day, and, when the preparation for teaching is more demanding and the time in the classroom increases, the period set aside for research is squeezed. Moreover, many of you are at a stage in your lives when you experience not only the career challenges—writing articles that will establish you as a researcher, learning how best to communicate with your students—but also the demands and responsibilities (and joys!) of raising children. Although creative thinking about philosophical issues usually refreshes and enlivens teaching, just as teaching often opens up new questions for philosophical research, your days may be too loaded with other activities to allow very much of either form of synergy.

That is a serious loss. For, if you are lucky enough to have time for exploration, your teaching can even open up a new field, one to which you may devote years. I had that good fortune. Almost at the beginning of my teaching career, a student at the University of Vermont changed the direction of my writing. Somewhat diffidently, he came to see me in office hours, to tell me that the students in my philosophy of science class were, like him, mostly premeds, and that they would appreciate some examples from biology. I was too ashamed to confess that I was utterly ignorant about this area of science, but his plea did prod me to visit the library, where I discovered David Hull's recently published introductory volume (Hull 1974—probably the most important text in inspiring the development of philosophy of biology). I started reading and was hooked. It led me to a program of wide reading in biology, to many long sessions with biologist colleagues, to a sabbatical at Harvard's Museum of Comparative Zoology, and to writing a number of books and articles in this area of philosophy.

A very few people spend a lifetime as wonderful teachers of philosophy, without writing very much at all. Another small minority are prolific authors, although they never teach. For most, however, there is a useful interaction between the two parts of a philosophical career. You may well conclude that, without taking on both roles, you would not succeed in the one to which you devoted all your time.

Option two attempts to respond to that concern. Instead of abandoning research, you live a divided professional life. You recognize that, to teach philosophy at the level that satisfies you, in the way that you take to be most helpful to your students (and, possibly, to other audiences), you need an academic license. To buy and renew that license, you have to pay in the currency the profession demands. So, periodically, you will have to publish an article or two, to show you are still a card-carrying member of the professional philosophers' club. You don't like the genre, but you know how to play the game. You resolve to do that throughout your academic life.

You wonder, of course, if you can keep it up. Will the times at which you find paying your dues frustrating, unpleasant, even sickening, come to be frequent enough to provoke you to chuck it all in? Even if you are confident about your strength of will, you are still likely to feel unsatisfied. You probably want to contribute not only to the lives of those whom you teach but also to the advance of philosophy. Realistically, none of us can expect to do very much in this way—the changes most philosophical writing can inspire are small—but you want to try to leave your own mark. You *care* about philosophy. You would like to show how to think philosophically about a live social issue or to craft some partial synthesis. The hoops you must jump through to maintain your credentials detract from your ability to do the kind of research you passionately want to pursue. They take considerable time. And they sap your energy. Perhaps you also regard your professional writings as a kind of pretense, and your hours spent on them as exercises in mauvaise foi.

The research pressures of the world you inhabit are considerably more intense than those I experienced when I was starting out. During the course of your graduate training, you may have been advised by well-meaning mentors to send off a paper to a journal. If you heeded the advice, you have probably already felt the keen sting of disappointment that comes from rejection, whether it arrived in the wake of a curt form letter, or was provoked by lengthy reports, parts of which you found uncomprehending and other sections that appeared gratuitously snide. Sometimes, of course, even negative referees can be generous and constructive. Even so, almost every philosopher, no matter how high the reputation, goes through this kind of "blooding." And it proves painful.

You may well wonder whether your skin is thick enough to enable you to compete in a contest in which some of your rivals, especially those who succeed early and often, appear completely attuned to the conventions of the profession, already adepts at "core philosophy" with impressive publications in "top journals." In the race for jobs, run each year with, it seems, a diminishing stock of prizes, they are a lap or two ahead.

Option two does work for some people. Some contemporary philosophers (including some I have referred to in the previous chapters) can wear different hats at different times, enabling them to combine satisfying teaching with two kinds of research, the dues-paying variety and the species they really want to do. But, I suspect, you find this option, too, unsatisfactory.

It has an obvious relative, toward which I have gestured in some of my previous attempts to address the issues you raise. Hold your nose and play by the rules. Do what the profession expects of you until you have a secure position. Then you can begin to write the kinds of philosophy you view as genuinely important. Your career will divide into two periods: an apprenticeship in which you must meet standards set by others, and an independent life when you become your own boss.

This version is, I think, superior to its predecessors. A few years of bowing to standards whose worth you question isn't too much of a burden. It is, after all, one borne by many laboratory scientists, who have to spend lengthy postdocs working on someone else's projects. (Although, it must be recognized, as the time demanded before job security is granted increases, the biological clock ticks ever more loudly for women who hope to begin a family.) For those who can reconcile them with their other aspirations, apprenticeships are typically valuable. They develop technique—as with musicians who undergo rigorous training, playing études before they perform the masterpieces of the repertoire. You could regard the professionally approved articles you publish before earning job security as an opportunity to sharpen the tools you will then deploy in your "proper work."

Nevertheless, you might reasonably wonder how the colleagues who have vigorously supported your early career, offering comments on drafts of your journal papers, perhaps even testifying to those with the authority to make your position permanent, will react when the early spate of publications in "core philosophy" dries up, and you start to dabble in more "peripheral" matters. Will you become an exile, labeled as dead wood? Will their dissatisfactions be expressed in attempts to impose a heavy teaching load—"After all, your *'research'* isn't doing anything to help our department"? Will some higher administrator listen to pleas to transfer you to some other unit (not of your own choosing)? Even if none of these measures succeeds, will the lack of local appreciation come to weigh on you?

I suspect you want not simply a job and a salary, but some kind of recognition, some confirmation that you, too, are contributing to intellectual life and to the mission of the university. It is possible that you may find colleagues in other departments. You may find your niche in a Humanities program. Perhaps you may come to be seen by other Humanities faculty as "the philosopher we can talk to."

You can increase your chances of a comfortable academic life by mixing some features of the second option into the approach of the third. Why must the switch from Orthodox Professional Philosopher to Doing Real Philosophy (your version), or to Dilettantish Popularizer (one of the labels your colleagues might use), be so dramatic? Perhaps, while your employment is still not secure, you might accompany your respectable articles with a piece of writing in the vein you intend to mine later? And, even after you are launched on your excavations, you might come back to the surface from time to time, to show that you can still chop logic with the best of them? One way to live happily ever after is a hybrid option (I'll consider it as a subcategory of option three). You engage in a significant amount of interdisciplinary writing and teaching, working with colleagues in other departments, in the Humanities in particular. You continue to publish in "mainstream" journals, albeit at a slower rate (not letting your professional philosophical friends know that you see this as a "leisure activity," something you take up when a currently fashionable game strikes your fancy). More and more, your time is taken up with your main work, and you write to make the kind of impact William James, John Dewey, and I want philosophy once again to have. Even if your colleagues lament the decreased productivity from your earlier years, you still wear the mask of respectability— and, they may concede, all your cross-departmental connections mark you out as an excellent university citizen, one whose broader reputation is even helpful to the philosophy department.

Yet any attempt to conform to the norms currently governing our profession, while also trying to make space for synthetic
philosophy, faces a difficulty I have not so far mentioned. You are
probably well aware of it. The problem consists in finding time
(and energy) to engage in two distinct kinds of reading. Many of
those who succeed in placing their submissions in the pages of
"the top journals" seem to read very little except "the latest literature on the topic" of their article. What they write is impressively
scholarly, studded with references to the previous contributions of
the coterie to which they aspire to belong (or in which they hope
to retain their position). Every wrinkle of "the most recent discussions" is acknowledged. They have dug deep, pored again and
again over the suggestions and arguments of their peers and their
rivals. Hours have been spent on a narrow program of highly specialized study.

Many years ago, an eminent philosopher remarked to me that
the great privilege of being a philosopher was the license to read
anything. He was right. The giants of the past have delighted in
using that license. As I've explored parts of the history of philosophy, I've been constantly astonished by the range of the reading of
some of our predecessors—not only the obvious suspects (Kant
and Mill) but also Rousseau (conversant with the latest zoology as
well as music theory) and Schopenhauer (an avid student of Indian
thought and a reader of the *Lancet*). Synthetic philosophy—
indeed, any venture employing *modus Cartwright*—demands
breadth of reading. Attentive to human life, with its diversity
of problems and potentialities, you may find yourself drawn to
genres far beyond what your professional competitors consider as
the proper bounds of philosophy—to works of anthropology and

history, even to poetry, drama, and novels. If you are dedicated to pursuing philosophy in this way, will you be able to combine the two styles, to do well enough not to be outcompeted by those for whom a handful of journals offer the only "indispensable" reading? Can you avoid falling between two stools?

Perhaps you can. Something akin to a hybrid strategy can work. It seems to be the life I have lived. At least, as others often see it. Like a few other philosophers I know, I appear to have walked a fine line, doing just enough "respectable" work to count as orthodox. With some weird stuff on the side.

In fact, I can't claim to have devised some clever strategy for pursuing the approach to philosophy I recommended in the foregoing chapters. I am a slow learner. It has taken me decades to develop the views I have presented here. Forty years ago, I was no rebel against the analytic philosophy I had only partially learned, and at which I have never been truly adept. Indeed, as I look back to the 1970s and early 1980s, it seems to me that the divergence of "core philosophy" from issues of broader concern was less pronounced. Professional Anglophone philosophy then was closer to other academic disciplines. It was easier to love.

My route to my present views was a series of accidents. The first, already described, turned me toward the philosophy of biology. A second occurred when a bout of flu led me to flip through *TV Guide*, where my eyes lit upon an advertisement, featuring a free book, a Creationist tract entitled *The Remarkable Birth of Planet Earth*. I wrote off, it arrived, and I read it. Finding it both an intellectual mess and so slick as to be plausible, I decided that its confusions—and those of a whole genre of anti-evolutionary manifestoes—ought to be thoroughly exposed. I began giving a few talks about the deep flaws in Creationism. The third accident occurred when, over lunch with Harry and Betty Stanton (the founders of Bradford Books), I casually mentioned what I had been doing. They immediately insisted that I must write a short book on the subject. *Abusing Science* (Kitcher 1982) was the outcome of that conversation, written in the following months, and published very quickly thereafter.

Few philosophers feel contempt for those who take up the cudgels on this kind of issue. Or for those who write about the overreach of human sociobiology, or about the ethical and social implications of the Human Genome Project, or about "intelligent design," or about the dangers of scientism, or about debates over what to do about climate change. I have had it *very* easy. As do many philosophers of science. There are plenty of places at which pieces of scientific research have an impact on public policies and thus on human lives. Philosophers who write on these topics will not be dismissed as having abandoned the discipline. They are seen as using their philosophical training in valuable ways, even though it isn't "core philosophy." And, of course, if they sometimes publish articles in "mainstream journals," that adds to the aura of respectability.

No cunning plan, laid out in advance. Lots of luck, with, at the end, an emerging perspective on what philosophy is and what it should be. The hybrid option will work—if your interests lie in particular directions, and if you enjoy sufficiently large doses of good fortune.

My fourth option attempts to generalize from the hybrid approach. It looks for philosophical fields in which questions arise that have an impact on people's lives and also are likely to be regarded as contributing to philosophy's mission. Philosophy of science, as I have said, is one obvious place where this can happen. But it is not the only possibility.

Some other locations: Philosophy of/in Art, Normative Ethics, Social Philosophy, Philosophy of Technology, Philosophy of Education, Political Philosophy. Although these are not the most central parts of philosophy (according to the orthodox), they are established enough. Most philosophy departments acknowledge a need to have someone who can "cover" these fields—although one or two of them might be more dispensable than the rest. If you choose one or more as your area(s) of specialization, you can discover potential investigations to last you a lifetime, without incurring dismissal by your colleagues. They may view you as less central than themselves. But you are not beyond the pale.

If you share my view about the importance of work in synthetic philosophy, and accept my characterization of it, the history of philosophy supplies rich choices. Turning to the past and focusing on a wide-ranging synthetic philosopher, you can attempt to develop that philosopher's perspective in ways that speak to our times. Your life can be profitably spent on a version of neo-Aristotelianism or neo-Kantianism (should it be neo-neo-Kantianism?). Or you may rescue the thought of an intellectual figure who has fallen out of the canon: Cicero, say, or Montaigne, or Dilthey. Through renewing a large perspective from the past, you may offer contemporary people new ways of conceiving their lives.

One form of this strategy consists in identifying an aspect of life today about which there is widespread puzzlement. Sex, for example. Birds do it, bees do it, human beings not only do it, but talk, think, and worry about it. Our times offer a whole complex of perplexities about how sexual relations should be initiated—between whom? under what prior conditions?—about the proper form of sex education, about pornography, and many more. Working from within one of the fields I have listed, or working across them, drawing on normative ethics, social philosophy, and political philosophy, you can attempt to clear up some of the chaos occurring throughout a sizeable chunk of the body underneath the hat (or the hair).

Amia Srinivasan has done this to great acclaim (Srinivasan 2021). Her writings are informed by large amounts of empirical information (a similarity with work in the philosophy of science). Her analyses and syntheses are astute and often surprising. Her prose combines the clarity of analytic philosophy at its best (neither haze nor hypertrophy here) with stylistic elegance. So she achieves a wide audience, to whom she can bring focused social and political philosophy to address widely shared perplexities.

Nor is she dismissed as a philosophical lightweight. To the contrary. In a bold and brilliant move, Oxford University—not always prominent for being innovative in educational matters—elected her as Chichele Professor of Social and Political Theory. This is a chair in which she will continue an important intellectual tradition—to which she is the worthy heir.

Although you might reasonably wonder about the chances of emulating her striking success—it seems to require unusual conditions, that, unfortunately, only a very few can currently enjoy, lavish doses of "dumb luck"—Srinivasan can be the model for the most satisfactory of my options. Start with live issues that provoke puzzlement in a significant portion of the population (perhaps in members of some identifiable group, perhaps spread across all sorts of segments of society). Investigate what is known about the empirical issues underlying the perplexities. (When philosophy returns to "being about stuff," it's crucial to know your stuff. One of the reasons underlying the appreciation of "applied work" is the sense that the author, like Srinivasan, knows a lot of facts about the area under study and has devoted a great deal of effort to synthesizing them.) Offer a perspective for bringing the material to order.

If you can do all that, you may be able to sidestep the difficulties I have noted with my previous options.

Amia Srinivasan offers hope that, even in these demanding times, if they receive the right opportunities, young philosophers may undertake important projects and still find a splendid home within the academy. Should that be the sole niche in which you might pursue the style of philosophy you find valuable? Earlier parts of my proposals have brushed against other possibilities. I have, for example, envisaged doing philosophy with stronger or looser ties to a philosophy department, situating yourself within some broader program. At various stages of their careers, my six exemplary synthetic philosophers have done just that.

Besides Philosophy, the fields with which they have (or have had) academic affiliations include the following: African-American Studies (Appiah), Classics (Nehamas, Nussbaum), Comparative Literature (Appiah, Nehamas), Divinity (Nussbaum), Gender and Sexuality Studies (Appiah), Humanities (Nehamas), Humanities Engaging Social Science (Cartwright), Human Rights (Nussbaum), Law (Anderson, Appiah, Nussbaum), Philosophy of Natural and Social Science (Cartwright), Political Science (Nussbaum), South Asian Studies

(Nussbaum), and Women's Studies (Anderson). Although she has held Chairs in Philosophy during the past, Nussbaum's current primary appointment is as a Distinguished Professor in a major American Law School.

Neiman has taken a further step. In 2000, after working in Philosophy Departments at two famous universities, she left a Professorship at Tel Aviv University to become Director of the Einstein Forum in Berlin. This Institute, a major center of intellectual life in Germany, has given her a place from which to continue her philosophical work and to take it into the broader cultural world. Her writings have been widely read on both sides of the Atlantic, and, although she no longer has students, she interacts not only with a broad range of thinkers in a variety of fields but with a staff of productive scholars, who, like her, have chosen to pursue their writing careers outside a university.

A position in philosophy at some institution of higher education is not the only option. There are possibilities elsewhere—in other divisions of colleges and universities, and outside the educational sphere entirely. As the scramble for academic appointments becomes ever more intense, perhaps the latter course will attract more of you.

But, if you follow it, you are likely to hear whispers charging you with desertion. Disdainful voices, ever ready to produce sentences of the form "X has given up philosophy." Sneers of that kind are sometimes directed at people like my exemplars, people who devote their efforts to philosophical questions that overlap the interests of other scholars, and who spend time working with (and in) other departments. They occur more frequently if another discipline comes to be the philosopher's primary affiliation, and

become almost de rigueur if a brave thinker chooses to pursue philosophy outside the academy.

Nothing justifies these accusations except a narrow conception
of philosophy as an inward-turning discipline populated by highly
focused specialists who talk (excitedly) only to one another. It
seems never to have occurred to those who level the charges that
the vast majority of philosophers in the Western canon earned
their keep outside a university philosophy department. Some were
engaged as private tutors, others as diplomats, or as theologians
or clerics, mathematicians or scientists. A few were political revo-
lutionaries, one ground lenses, and one was a colonial administrator. The *psychology* building on the Harvard campus is named
for William James—philosophers dwell in Emerson hall, so called
after a man who was exiled from his alma mater for a large chunk
of his adult life. The catalog could be extended at length, to under-
score the irony of the accusatory mutterings. Has "core philosophy" lost all sense of humor?

If you decide to work in another academic discipline, or to work
outside a university, perhaps in some setting akin to the Einstein
Forum, you should be prepared for some hyper-professional analytic philosophers to say—probably behind your back—that you
"have given up real philosophy." Whether you hear it or not, the
gibe should have no sting. For the idea that the path you have chosen must lead you to desert philosophy is laughable. Dismissive
comments of this kind should be voiced only after a careful,
informed, and sensitive review of the work a scholar produces—
if they are uttered at all. Yet, if they are to be made, they should
rebound on those who standardly issue them. Some of the most
zealous and specialized apostles of core analytic philosophy have a

far stronger claim to the title of deserter. Isn't the narrowness and insularity of their productions a clear sign of having abandoned the great philosophical tradition?

I do not think what I have said so far touches the deepest source of your concerns. For it leaves in place many features of the status quo. As I hear you, you do not simply want to carve out a life in which you can do the work you want, having a satisfactory career within a philosophical world run according to a particular conception, and imposing particular standards. Or to leave it, and work elsewhere, on terms of peaceful coexistence with the professional orthodoxy. You want to change the conception and replace the standards. Even if "core philosophers" come to recognize the value of what you do, you don't want the prevailing notion of what "core philosophy" is to remain in place. Perhaps (like the author who wrote the original version of Chapter 1) you would like to turn philosophy inside out. Or maybe (as I hope) you share the present author's wish that the pathologies will be cured, the distinction between core and periphery abolished, and the philosophical venture regain its power to have an intellectual impact, through its direct contributions to resolving particular live issues *and* through its partial syntheses. In the end, it's not just about your life. It's about the future of the discipline you love.

As I said in my reply to that first questioner, and have said on several occasions since, it's the responsibility of senior members of the profession who have arrived (sometimes, as I have, in chancy and muddled ways) at the views I have outlined here, to do what they can to amend the norms and conventions of the profession, the constraints that bind, under which you chafe. To "play the game" or to "go under cover" or even to follow my fourth option would not count as a full solution. The point is not just to understand the state of the Anglophone philosophy profession. It is to change it.

How can that be done? Hastening to the barricades to demonstrate against the philosophical establishment is not likely to succeed. Defenders of the current professionalization will use the skills they deploy in their professional work to eviscerate the demonstrators—or to carry out what they, and those who are like-minded, can claim to be evisceration. We do better, I think, to build on some of the developments of the past decade to create— *together*—an academic environment in which the kind of work you hope to do can be supported, in which its worth—and its attractions—will become ever more visible.

In my opening fantasy, the breakaway pianists who desert the étude Olympics to perform classics (and, perhaps, some newly written pieces) for an appreciative audience only elicit even more disdainful sniffs from the cognoscenti. That is not the inevitable end of the story, although it may well be a passing phase. Continued acclaim for "popular concerts" could slowly begin an exodus. Not only does the noncompeting audience for further assaults on *Multiple Tremolo 41* disappear entirely, but, each year, the number of competitors diminishes. Eventually, disdain proves hard to sustain. Only the diehards resist joining their fellows who receive the adulation of the slums.

As the previous chapter noted, the past ten years have witnessed a shift. More philosophers have begun to write for a broader public. Their ranks include some established figures, people whose writings on "core topics" have been much admired. I gave a very short list (the first few people who came to my mind) in the previous chapter, but there are many more, people whose work you know better than I do, and whose writings may have given you encouragement. Inspired by this trend, those who would like to see philosophy regain its place in the wider culture might band together, start a movement to plead for institutional changes, at first on a modest scale. The acknowledgment of "public philosophy" as an important part of what philosophers do could be expressed in the funding of centers to support scholars—especially younger scholars—so they could have time to develop their contributions to this genre. Fellowships for one year or for two years would be a start.

A campaign to enrich philosophical culture could begin there. It should aspire, however, to go *much* further. Centers of this kind might invest in longer-term support. The seven years of an All Souls' Prize Fellowship—under which Amia Srinivasan was given time to think through her ideas—provide a model for nurturing more ambitious ventures in synthetic philosophy. The status quo does not have to be overthrown overnight. Its limitations may become evident as alternatives to the current professional style become ever more diverse and ever more visible.

If these limited ventures succeed, more ambitious reforms may follow. Philosophy is currently an isolated discipline within a larger cluster of academic fields, the always-besieged low-status areas universities call "the Humanities." As philosophers emerge who can begin to engage with their colleagues from other parts of this culture, philosophy contributes to a valuable general program in the Humanities—philosophers participate in a curriculum in which the synthetic enterprises of philosophy's past are given their due. Such programs enlighten those who teach, as well as those whose official role is that of student. Rereading classic works of philosophy *in conjunction with* texts from other areas in the Humanities prompts a Gestalt switch. Even the most dedicated "core philosopher" finds it difficult to resist viewing the subject differently.

It is no accident, I think, that the department in which I have spent the last twenty (happy) years is full of people whose writings (sometimes) find readers from other academic disciplines and beyond the academy as well. Teaching in Columbia's program of general education (the "Columbia core"), as most of us have done, undermines the insular vision of philosophy as a segregated business. Certainly, in my own case, the years I have spent teaching sophomores for whom "Contemporary Civilization" is required, as well as helping to train the graduate preceptors who have responsibility for some sections of the course, have broadened my philosophical sympathies and modified my approach to my profession. Like M. Jourdain, who learned that he had been speaking prose all his life, I discovered that I had always been a pragmatist and a would-be synthetic philosopher.

Hence, a further step. Amend my fantasy of the Dean or Provost who dismisses philosophy as useless—and then dismisses the philosophers. Our administrator takes note of the current isolation of the philosophy department. But there are a few promising signs of rapprochement with other parts of the university. In particular, one or two philosophy faculty are collaborating with other colleagues in the Humanities, and they are writing on topics of public concern, in ways the administrator finds valuable. After conversations with several faculty members in the Humanities division comes a decision to institute a new Humanities course. Or, perhaps, a center for public philosophy. Maybe even to appoint someone to teach, and to do research in, public philosophy. Or to do synthetic philosophy.

So philosophy starts to rejoin the division within which it has lived, for decades now, in inner exile. If this administrator runs your university or college, you begin to have, at least locally, the reshaping of philosophy you would like to see.

Your administrator talks to opposite numbers at different academic institutions. Some of those conversations report academic successes. Others are inspired to emulate what has been done. Across the English-speaking world, there are gradual changes. More appointments in the kinds of philosophy you aspire to do. A different composition of philosophy departments and of the philosophy profession. Even if a significant population of die-hards remains, resolutely breaking records for *Multiple Tremolo 41*, that is no longer a concern for you or for your philosophical kin. The holdouts can be left to play the games that interest and amuse them. For you and those like you form a sufficiently large company to pursue projects of a very different kind.

To try to renew philosophy.

The gradual evolution of our subject I have outlined suggests the ways in which established philosophers can seek changes. Perhaps some of you may be able to envisage ways in which the process could be accelerated. (If so, I would like to know about your ideas.) Urging reform along these lines is, so far as I can tell, the best strategy for facilitating progressive change in the profession of philosophy in the Anglophone world. So I offer this program, tentatively, as a supplement to my models of how you might aim for a satisfying career within a field whose current norms you find constraining.

Of course, there is another, very obvious, way of trying to change the culture of philosophy. You can write books about the character of philosophy. Like this one. Or, I hope, better ones. They might lead people to rethink what they have been doing. Alternatively, such uncomprehending manifestoes could cause well-socialized readers to dig in their heels and to write broadsides against philistinism. Engendering philosophical debates, in which each side tacitly appeals to its own standards.

Yet however those debates unfold, however frustrating they appear, staking out a position at some length can help a nascent community of rebels to form. The banner may be poorly designed and poorly woven, left tattered by the barrage of shells directed at it—but its continued fluttering in the winds may have a valuable effect. It can serve to bring together people drawn to a common cause. And thus help promote a collective effort at reform.

I have written this book to try to change minds. It may do some of that (if, as I have so often been, I am lucky). But I would not have written it without the encouragement I have received from you and from others like you. Your questions and comments have given me a little hope that my vision is not entirely idiosyncratic. And hence that presenting it, as I have done here, is not an utter waste of time.

So, thank you. I hope these brief remarks are of some help. More than that, I trust that you will have the philosophical life to which you aspire, and that, through your efforts, the philosophy of the future may attain, once again, the glories of its past.

Good luck.

NOTES

CHAPTER I

1. My case is restricted to philosophy in the English-speaking world. Some non-Anglophone traditions seem healthier. I think, for example, of Frankfurt School critical theory, especially as developed by Jürgen Habermas, Axel Honneth, and Rahel Jaeggi.

2. I follow other authors, especially Bernard Williams, in distinguishing between morality and ethics. Morality is concerned with action: its central question is "What should I do?" Ethics is broader, asking "What kind of person should I be?" It is more inclusive than morality, since acting rightly is necessary (but not sufficient) for being ethically good.

CHAPTER 2

1. As noted in the Preface, my references to particular authors, whom I associate with positive developments, are intended merely to point to instances of various general types. It would be foolish to claim that my choices are the only exemplars, or even the best ones. Others would select differently, and I would expect broad agreement on the value of a far lengthier list.

CHAPTER 3

1. Perhaps the author would be inclined to imitate Shakespeare's Cassius:

> The fault, dear Reader, is not in my claim,
> But in yourself, that intuition's dim.

2. Perhaps evolutionary debunkers will contend that this is not the challenge they intend to level. "We're concerned," they may say, "with the selective advantage of a *whole* moral sense. What's the use of that?" To which the obvious reply is: "In which environment? If you are talking about a world—like ours—in which people with defective capacities of this kind are condemned and socially sanctioned, there are some pretty obvious advantages of having the capacity moral realists ascribe. The real issue, then, is how an environment of that type came to be, how a significantly large majority of the human population came to be able to make and act on correct moral judgments and to expect their fellows to conform to them. Hence, your question is a historical one, focused on how an embryonic power of detection caught on sufficiently widely to make that kind of environment possible. So you are asking the same question as the higher end versions of Creationism, while remaining lamentably vague about the specifics. And offering the same cheap gibe."

REFERENCES

Akerlof, George. 1984. "The Market for Lemons: Quality, Uncertainty, and the Market Mechanism." In *An Economic Theorist's Book of Tales*, 7–22. Cambridge: Cambridge University Press.

Albert, David. 1992. *Quantum Mechanics and Experience*. Cambridge, MA: Harvard University Press.

Anderson, Elizabeth. 2010. *The Imperative of Integration*. Princeton, NJ: Princeton University Press.

Anderson, Elizabeth. 2017. *Private Government*. Princeton, NJ: Princeton University Press.

Appiah, Kwame Anthony. 1992. *In My Father's House*. New York: Oxford University Press.

Appiah, Kwame Anthony. 2006. *The Ethics of Identity*. Princeton, NJ: Princeton University Press.

Appiah, Kwame Anthony. 2018. *The Lies That Bind*. New York: Norton/Liveright.

Barnes, Barry. 1977. *Interests and the Growth of Knowledge*. London: Routledge and Kegan Paul.

Carnap, Rudolf. 1928. *Scheinprobleme in der Philosophie*. Berlin: Weltkreis-Verlag.

Cartwright, Nancy. 1983. *How the Laws of Physics Lie*. Oxford: Oxford University Press.

Cartwright, Nancy. 1999. *The Dappled World*. Cambridge: Cambridge University Press.

Cartwright, Nancy. 2007. *Hunting Causes and Using Them*. Cambridge: Cambridge University Press.

Cavell, Stanley. 1969. *Must We Mean What We Say?* New York: Scribner's.

Churchland, Patricia. 2019. *Conscience.* New York: W.W. Norton.

Collins, Harry. 1985. *Changing Order.* London: Sage.

Danto, Arthur. 1964. "The Artworld." *Journal of Philosophy* 61: 571–584.

Danto, Arthur. 1981. *The Transfiguration of the Commonplace.* Cambridge, MA: Harvard University Press.

Danto, Arthur. 1997. *After the End of Art.* Princeton, NJ: Princeton University Press.

Dewey, John. (1909) 1998. "The Influence of Darwin on Philosophy." In *John Dewey, The Middle Works*, Vol. 4, 3–14. Carbondale: University of Southern Illinois.

Dewey, John. (1916) 1980. *Democracy and Education.* Carbondale: University of Southern Illinois. 1980 reprinting of the 1916 original as *John Dewey, The Middle Works*, vol. 9.

Dewey, John. (1920) 1982. *Reconstruction in Philosophy.* Carbondale: University of Southern Illinois. 1982 reprinting of the 1920 original as *John Dewey, The Middle Works*, vol. 12.

Dewey, John. (1925) 1981. *Experience and Nature.* Carbondale: University of Southern Illinois Press. 1981 reprinting of the 1925 original as *John Dewey: The Later Works*, vol. 1.

Dewey, John. (1929) 1988. *The Quest for Certainty.* Carbondale: University of Southern Illinois Press. 1988 reprinting of the 1929 original as *John Dewey: The Later Works*, vol. 4.

Dewey, John. (1934) 1986. *A Common Faith.* Carbondale: University of Southern Illinois Press. 1986 reprinting of the 1934 original as *John Dewey: The Later Works*, vol. 9.

Douglas, Heather. 2009. *Science, Policy, and the Value-Free Ideal.* Pittsburgh: University of Pittsburgh Press.

Dupré, John. 1993. *The Disorder of Things.* Cambridge MA: Harvard University Press.

Dupré, John. 2001. *Human Nature and the Limits of Science.* Oxford: Oxford University Press.

Elgin, Catherine. 2017. *True Enough.* Cambridge, MA: MIT Press.

Feyerabend, Paul. 1978. *Science in a Free Society*. London: New Left Books.

Feyerabend, Paul. 1987. *Farewell to Reason*. London: Verso/New Left Books.

Fine, Arthur. 1988. "Interpreting Science." *PSA: Proceedings of the Biennial Meetings of the Philosophy of Science Association* 1988, no. 2: 3–11.

Foot, Philippa. 1967. "The Problem of Abortion and the Doctrine of Double Effect." *Oxford Review* 5. Reprinted in *Virtues and Vices*. Berkeley: University of California Press, 1978.

Frege, Gottlob. (1884) 1968. *The Foundations of Arithmetic*. Oxford: Blackwell.

Fricker, Miranda. 2007. *Epistemic Injustice*. Oxford: Oxford University Press.

Friedman, Michael. 1974. "Explanation and Scientific Understanding." *Journal of Philosophy* 71: 5–19.

Godfrey-Smith, Peter. 2016. *Other Minds: The Octopus, the Sea, and the Deep Origins of Consciousness*. New York: Farrar, Straus, Giroux.

Godfrey-Smith, Peter. 2020. *Metazoa: Animal Minds and the Birth of Consciousness*. New York: Farrar, Straus, Giroux.

Goehr, Lydia. 2007. *The Imaginary Museum of Musical Works*. New York: Oxford University Press.

Goldman, Alvin. 1999. *Knowledge in a Social World*. New York: Oxford University Press.

Graham, Patricia Albjerg. 2005. *Schooling America*. Oxford: Oxford University Press.

Gross, Paul, and Norman Levitt. 1994. *Higher Superstition*. Baltimore: Johns Hopkins University Press.

Hardy, G. H. 1967. *A Mathematician's Apology*. Cambridge: Cambridge University Press.

Hegselmann, Rainer, and Ulrich Krause. 2002. "Opinion Dynamics and Bounded Confidence Models, Analysis, and Simulation." *Journal of Artificial Societies and Social Simulation* 5, no. 3. https://www.jasss.org/5/3/2.html.

Hempel, C. G. 1950. "Problems and Changes in the Empiricist Criterion of Meaning." *Revue Internationale de Philosophie* 41: 41–63.

Hempel, C. G. 1951. "The Concept of Cognitive Significance: A Reconsideration." *Proceedings of the American Academy of Arts and Sciences* 80: 61–77.

Hempel, C. G. 1965. *Aspects of Scientific Explanation and Other Essays.* New York: The Free Press.

Hull, David. 1974. *Philosophy of Biological Science.* Englewood Cliffs, NJ: Prentice-Hall.

James, William. (1879) 1979. "The Sentiment of Rationality." In *The Will to Believe*, 36–60. Cambridge MA: Harvard University Press.

James, William. (1904) 1978. "The Pragmatic Method." *Journal of Philosophy* 1: 673–687; in William James, *Essays in Philosophy*, 123–139. Cambridge, MA: Harvard University Press, 1978.

James, William. (1907) 1975. *Pragmatism.* Cambridge, MA: Harvard University Press.

Kant, Immanuel. (1787) 1996. *Critique of Pure Reason.* Translated by Werner Pluhar. Indianapolis: Hackett.

Keller, Evelyn Fox. 1985. *Reflections on Gender and Science.* New Haven, CT: Yale University Press.

Kitcher, Philip. 1980. "*A Priori* Knowledge." *Philosophical Review* 79: 3–23.

Kitcher, Philip. 1981. "Explanatory Unification." *Philosophy of Science* 48: 507–531.

Kitcher, Philip. 1982. *Abusing Science: The Case Against Creationism.* Cambridge, MA: MIT Press.

Kitcher, Philip. 1985. *Vaulting Ambition: Sociobiology and the Quest for Human Nature.* Cambridge, MA: MIT Press.

Kitcher, Philip. 1993. *The Advancement of Science.* New York: Oxford University Press.

Kitcher, Philip. 1996. *The Lives to Come.* New York: Simon & Schuster.

Kitcher, Philip. 2001. *Science, Truth, and Democracy.* New York: Oxford University Press.

Kitcher, Philip. 2007. *Living with Darwin.* New York: Oxford University Press.

Kitcher, Philip. 2011. "Philosophy Inside Out." *Metaphilosophy* 42: 248–260.

Kitcher, Philip. 2011a. *The Ethical Project.* Cambridge, MA: Harvard University Press.

Kitcher, Philip. 2011b. *Science in a Democratic Society.* Amherst, NY: Prometheus Books.

Kitcher, Philip. 2021a. *Moral Progress*. New York: Oxford University Press.

Kitcher, Philip. 2021b. *The Main Enterprise of the World: Rethinking Education*. New York: Oxford University Press.

Kitcher, Philip, and Evelyn Fox Keller. 2017. *The Seasons Alter*. New York: Norton/Liveright.

Kuhn, T. S. 1962. *The Structure of Scientific Revolutions*. Chicago: University of Chicago Press.

Lakatos, Imre. 1970. "Falsificationism and the Methodology of Scientific Research Programmes." In *Criticism and the Growth of Knowledge*, edited by I. Lakatos and A. Musgrave, 91–196. Cambridge: Cambridge University Press.

Lange, Marc. 2017. *Because without Cause*. New York: Oxford University Press.

Latour, Bruno. 1987. *Science in Action*. Cambridge, MA: Harvard University Press.

Laudan, Larry. 1977. *Progress and its Problems*. Berkeley: University of California Press.

Levi, Isaac. 1974. "On Indeterminate Probabilities." *Journal of Philosophy* 71: 391–418.

Lewis, David. 1973. *Counterfactuals*. Oxford: Blackwell.

Lloyd, Elisabeth, and Eric Winsberg, eds. 2018. *Climate Modeling: Philosophical and Conceptual Issues*. London: Palgrave Macmillan.

Longino, Helen. 1990. *Science as Social Knowledge*. Princeton, NJ: Princeton University Press.

Mill, John Stuart. (1859) 2008. *On Liberty and Other Essays*. Oxford: Oxford University Press (World's Classics).

Morton, Jennifer M. 2020. *Moving Up Without Losing Your Way*. Princeton, NJ: Princeton University Press.

Munro, E., N. Cartwright, J. Hardie, and E. Montuschi. 2017. *Improving Child Safety: Deliberation, Judgement and Empirical Research*. Durham, UK: Centre for Humanities Engaging Science and Society.

Nehamas, Alexander. 1998. *The Art of Living*. Berkeley: University of California Press.

Nehamas, Alexander. 2007. *Only a Promise of Happiness*. Princeton, NJ: Princeton University Press.

Nehamas, Alexander. 2016. *On Friendship*. New York: Basic Books.

Neiman, Susan. 2002. *Evil in Modern Thought*. Princeton, NJ: Princeton University Press.

Neiman, Susan. 2008. *Moral Clarity*. Princeton, NJ: Princeton University Press.

Neiman, Susan. 2014. *Why Grow Up?* London: Penguin.

Neiman, Susan. 2019. *Learning from the Germans*. New York: Farrar, Straus, Giroux.

Nussbaum, Martha C. 2011. *Creating Capabilities*. Cambridge, MA: Harvard University Press.

Nussbaum, Martha C. 2012. *Women and Human Development*. Cambridge: Cambridge University Press.

Nussbaum, Martha C. 2015. *Political Emotions*. Cambridge, MA: Harvard University Press.

Nussbaum, Martha C. 2016. *Not for Profit*. Princeton, NJ: Princeton University Press.

O'Connor, Cailin, and James Weatherall. 2019. *The Misinformation Age*. New Haven, CT: Yale University Press.

Parfit, Derek. 1984. *Reasons and Persons*. Oxford: Oxford University Press.

Parfit, Derek. 2011. *On What Matters*. Two vols. Oxford: Oxford University Press.

Parker, Wendy. 2020. "Model Evaluation: An Adequacy-for-Purpose View." *Philosophy of Science* 87: 457–477.

Paul, Laurie. 2014. *Transformative Experience*. Oxford: Oxford University Press.

Pearl, Judaea. 2000. *Causality: Models, Reasoning, and Inference*. Cambridge: Cambridge University Press.

Peirce, Charles Sanders. (1868) 1974. "Some Consequences of Four Incapacities." In *Collected Papers of Charles Sanders Peirce*, edited by Charles Hartshorne and Paul Weiss, vol. V, 156–189. Cambridge, MA: Harvard University Press.

Peirce, Charles Sanders. (1878) 1974. "How to Make Our Ideas Clear." In *Collected Papers of Charles Sanders Peirce*, edited by Charles Hartshorne and Paul Weiss, vol. V, 248–271. Cambridge, MA: Harvard University Press.

Pippin, Robert. 2000. *Henry James and Modern Moral Life.* Cambridge: Cambridge University Press.

Popper, K. R. 1934. *Logik der Forschung.* Wien: Julius Springer.

Rawls, John. 1993. *Political Liberalism.* New York: Columbia University Press.

Rawls, John. 1999. *A Theory of Justice.* Revised edition. Cambridge, MA: Harvard University Press.

Salmon, Wesley. 1971. *Statistical Explanation and Statistical Relevance.* Pittsburgh: University of Pittsburgh Press.

Scheffler, Israel. 1967. *Science and Subjectivity.* Indianapolis: Bobbs-Merrill.

Schelling, Thomas. 1978. "Sorting and Mixing: Race and Sex." In his *Micromotives and Macrobehavior*, 135–166. New York: Norton.

Sellars, Wilfrid. 1963. *Science, Perception, and Reality.* London: Routledge and Kegan Paul.

Sen, Amartya. 1977. "Rational Fools." *Philosophy and Public Affairs* 6: 317–344.

Singer, Peter. 1972. "Famine, Affluence, and Morality." *Philosophy and Public Affairs* 1: 229–243.

Skyrms, Brian. 1996. *Evolution of the Social Contract.* Cambridge: Cambridge University Press.

Skyrms, Brian. 2004. *The Stag Hunt.* Cambridge: Cambridge University Press.

Sokal, Alan. 1996. "Transgressing the Boundaries: Toward a Transformative Hermeneutics of Quantum Gravity." *Social Text* 46/47: 217–252.

Spirtes, Peter, Clark Glymour, and Richard Scheines. 2000. *Causation, Predication, and Search.* Cambridge, MA: MIT Press.

Srinivasan, Amia. 2021. *The Right to Sex.* New York: Farrar, Straus, Giroux.

Stalnaker, Robert. 1968. "A Theory of Conditionals." In *Studies in Logical Theory*, edited by Nicholas Rescher, 98–112. Oxford: Blackwell.

Stanley, Jason. 2015. *How Propaganda Works.* Princeton, NJ: Princeton University Press.

Street, Sharon. 2006. "A Darwinian Dilemma for Realist Theories of Value." *Philosophical Studies* 127: 109–166.

Thomson, Judith Jarvis. 1971. "A Defense of Abortion." *Philosophy and Public Affairs* 1: 47–66.

Wilholt, Torsten. 2009. "Bias and Values in Scientific Research." *Studies in the History and Philosophy of Science* 40: 92–101.

Williams, Bernard. 1981. *Moral Luck*. Cambridge: Cambridge University Press.

Winsberg, Eric. 2018. *Philosophy and Climate Science*. New York: Cambridge University Press.

Woodward, James. 2003. *Making Things Happen*. New York: Oxford University Press.

Woodward, James. 2021. *Causation with a Human Face*. New York: Oxford University Press.